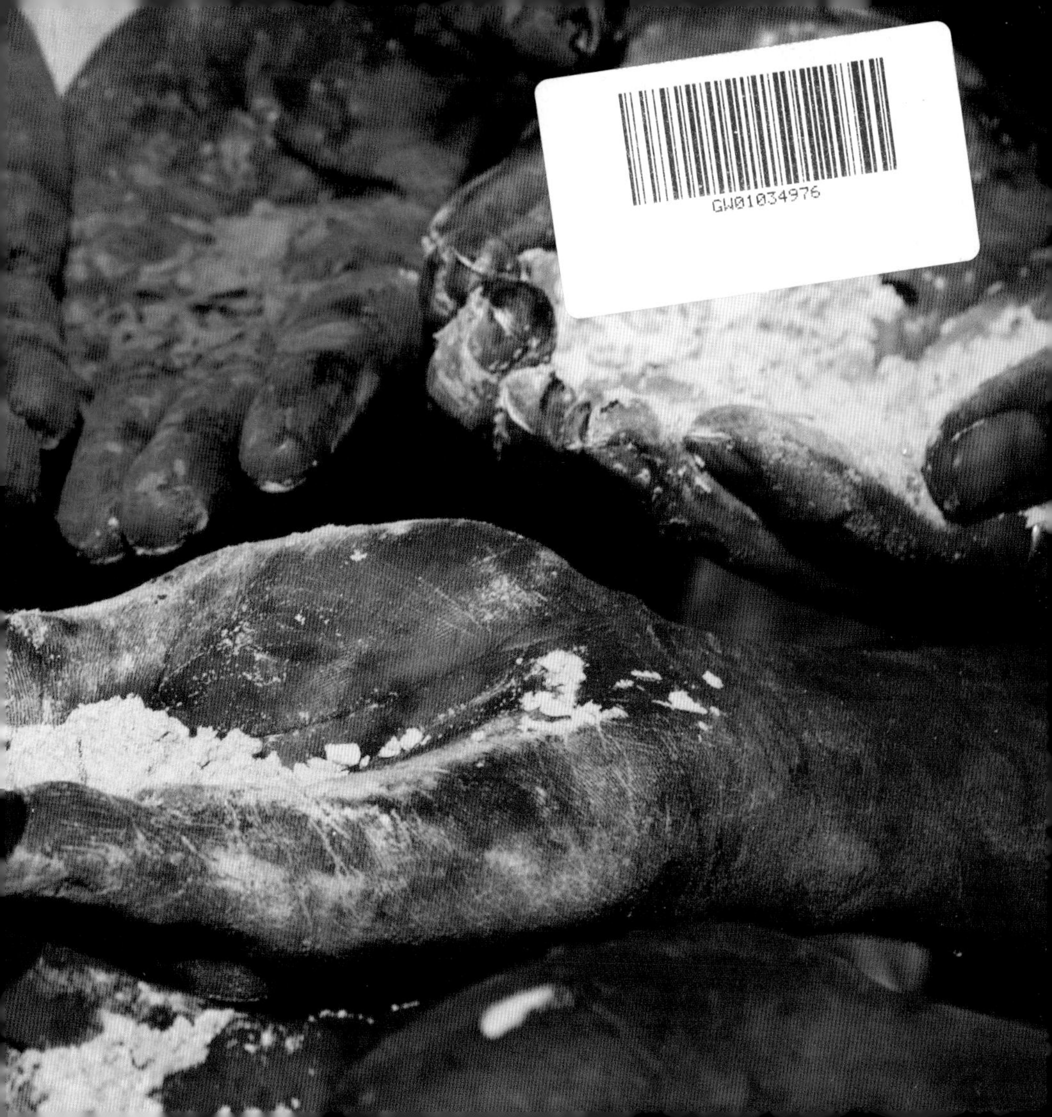

Affirmations
PUBLISHING HOUSE
living words

First published in 2010

Published by
Affirmations Publishing House
34 Hyde Street, Bellingen NSW 2454 Australia
t: +61 2 6655 2350
e: sales@affirmations.com.au
w: www.affirmations.com.au

Selection and design by Suzanne and Barbara Maher
Edited by Suzanne and Barbara Maher

10 9 8 7 6 5 4 3 2 1

ISBN 978-0-9808150-0-9

Printed in China on recycled paper using vegetable based inks.
Designed in Australia

While every effort has been made to acknowledge the author of the quotations used please contact the publisher if this has not occurred.

To Dearest Lurline

Affirmations are living words that bring meaning to life,
giving memories to share with everyone, everywhere.

Sounds you can see,
Colours you can feel,
Light you can hear.

Love Always

Audrey x

sisterhood

noun

The relationship between sisters.
The feeling of kinship and closeness to all women.
A community of women linked by common interests.

This one's for you Stacy,
my sister by choice.

SISTERS

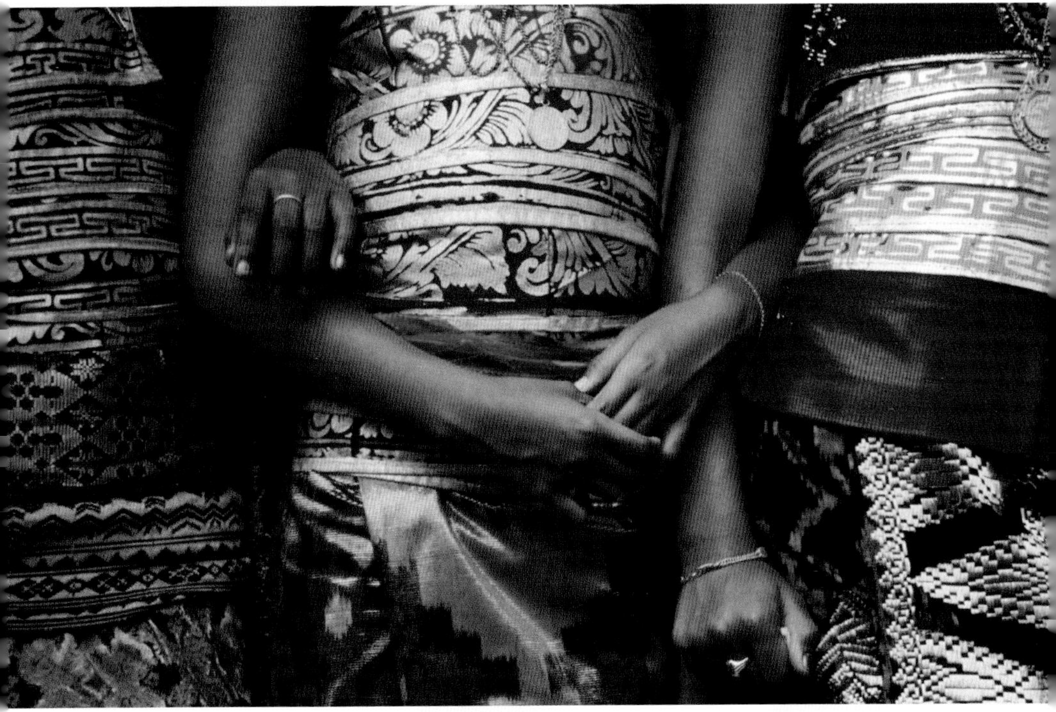

Designed by Suzanne and Barbara Maher

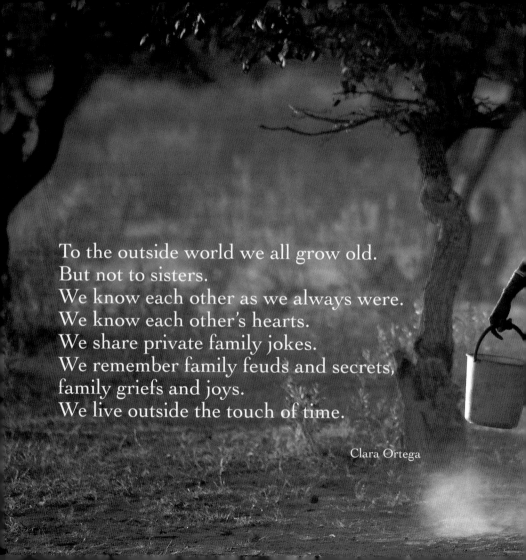

To the outside world we all grow old.
But not to sisters.
We know each other as we always were.
We know each other's hearts.
We share private family jokes.
We remember family feuds and secrets,
family griefs and joys.
We live outside the touch of time.

Clara Ortega

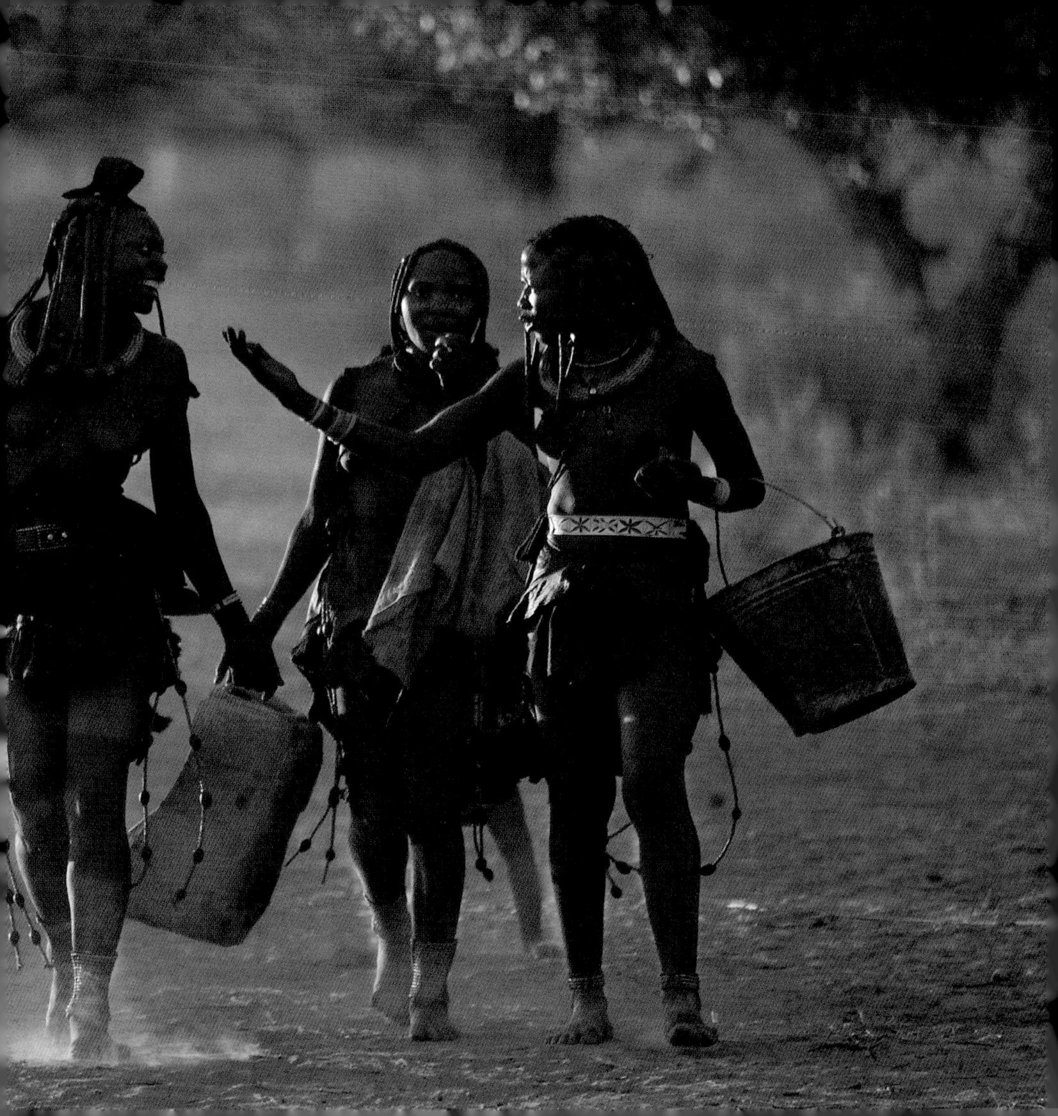

Sisters are different flowers

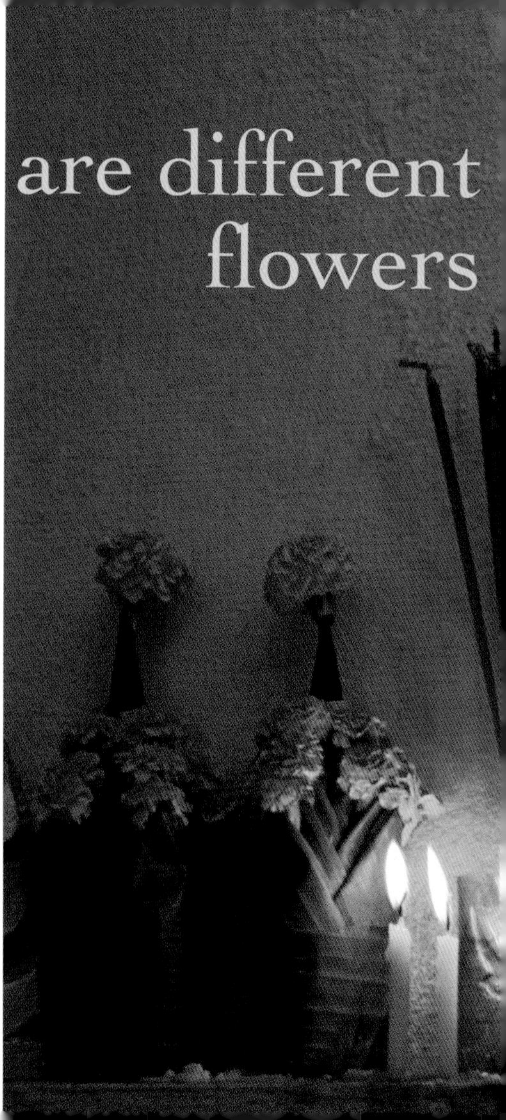

from the same garden.

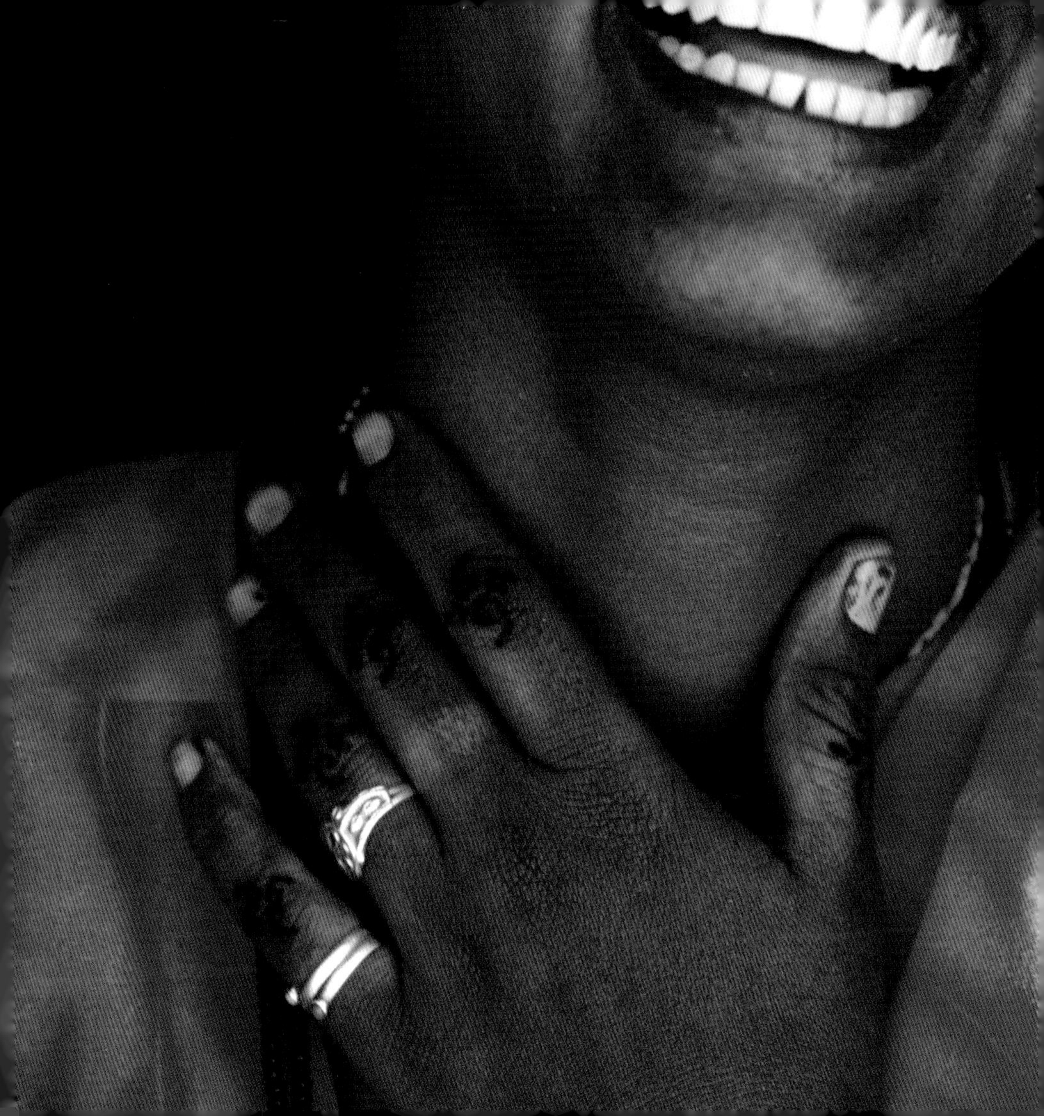

sweet

safe

steadfast

forgiving

dependable

connected

sympathetic

supportive

encouraging

caring

reassuring

understanding

concerned

helpful

kind

sister

connected for life

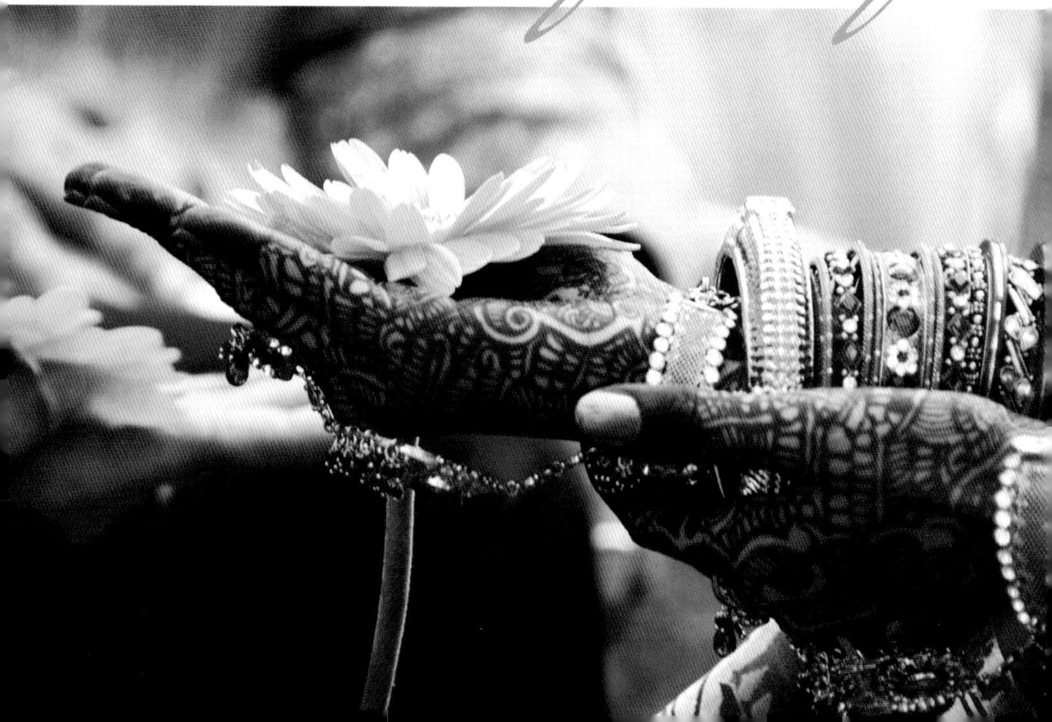

What greater joy is there
for human souls
than to feel that they are
connected for life -
to be with each other
in silent unspeakable memories.

George Eliot

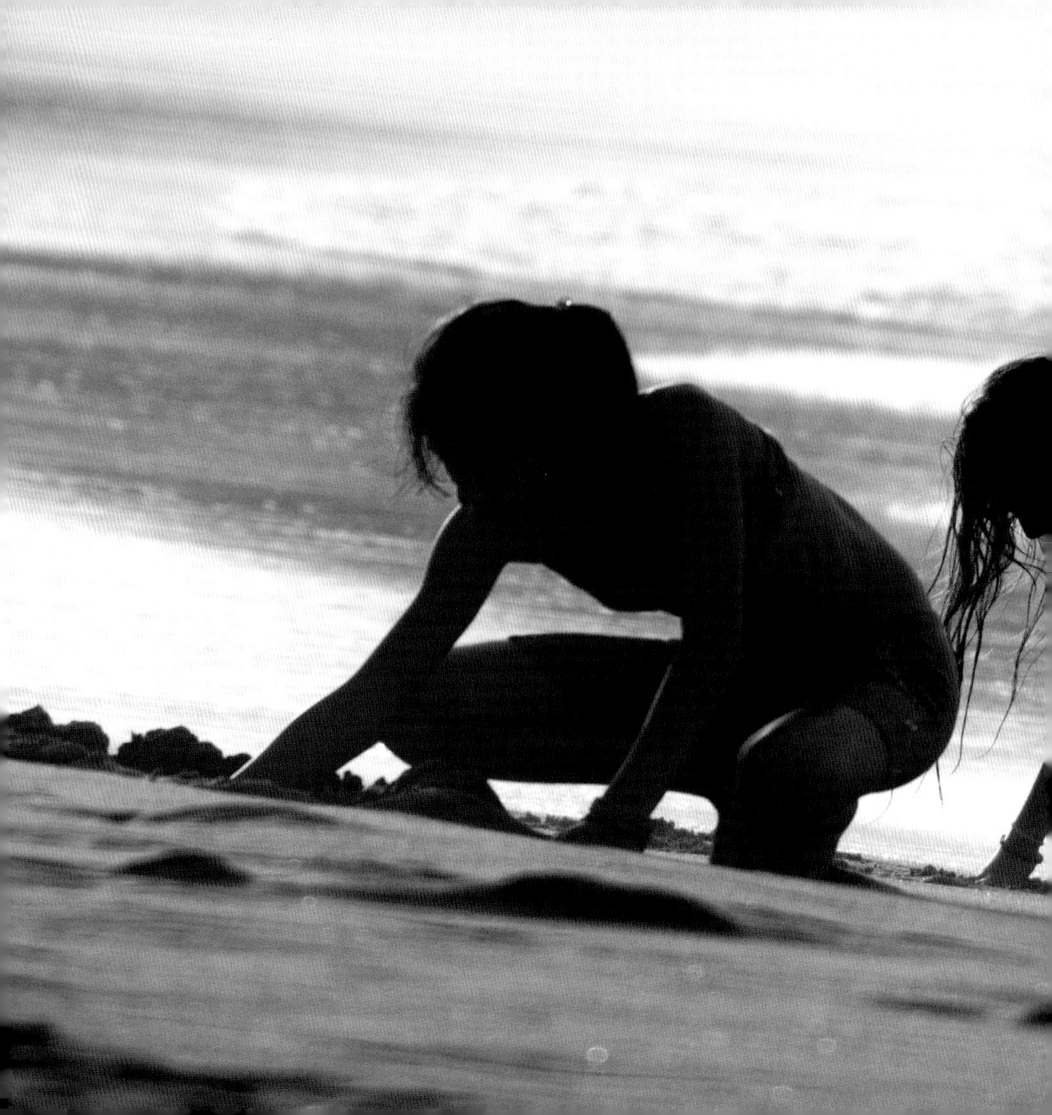

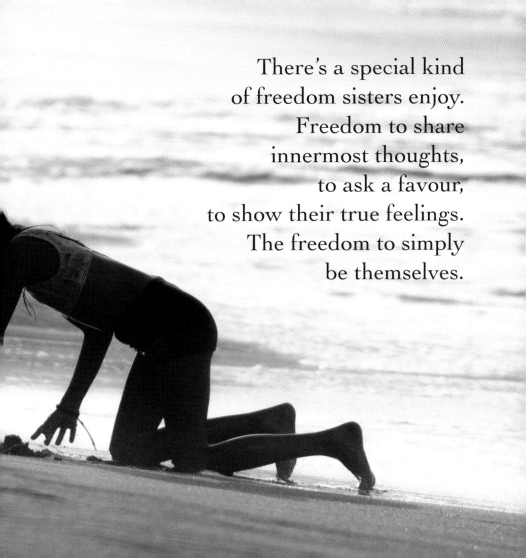

There's a special kind
of freedom sisters enjoy.
Freedom to share
innermost thoughts,
to ask a favour,
to show their true feelings.
The freedom to simply
be themselves.

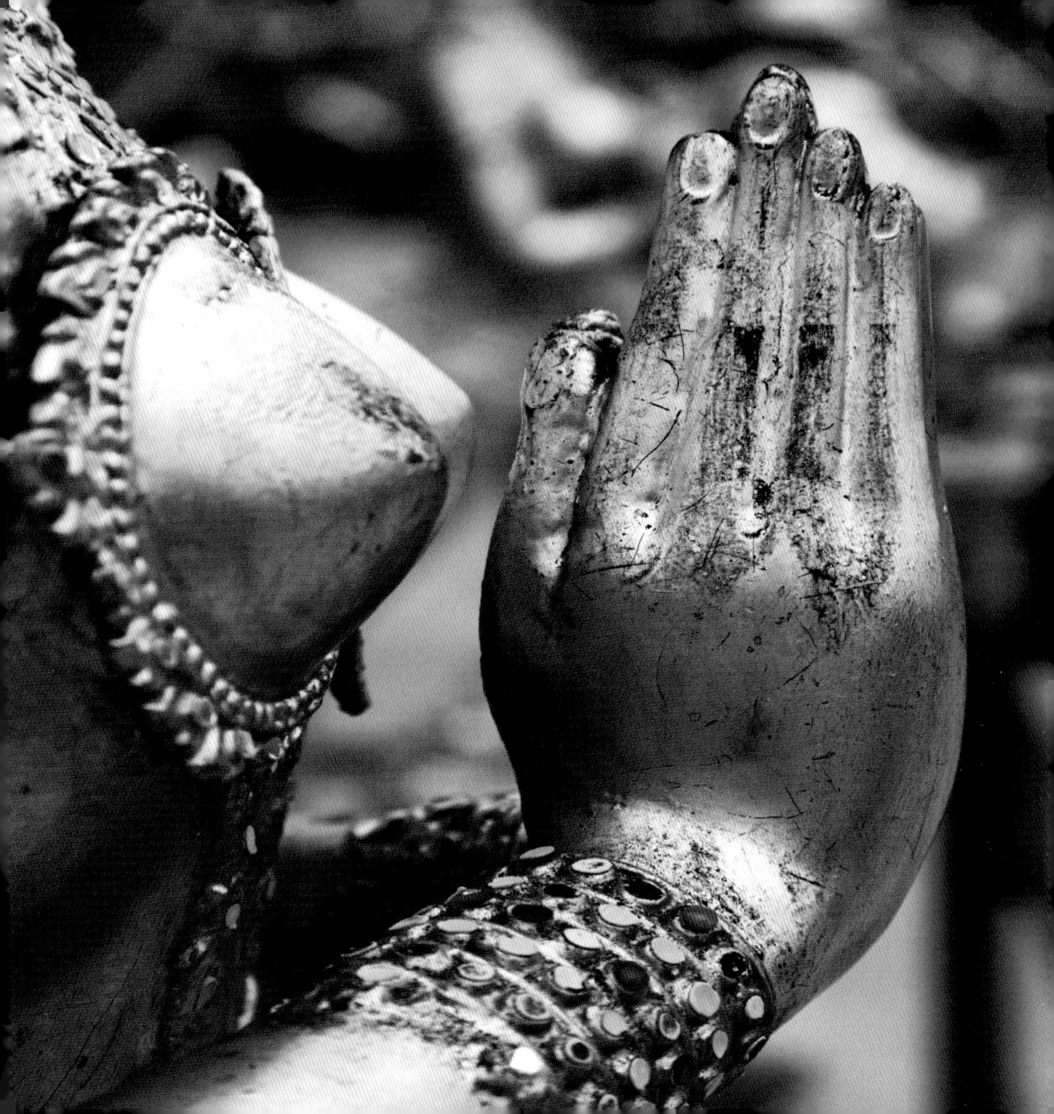

Help

one another

is part of

the religion of

sisterhood.

Louisa May Alcott

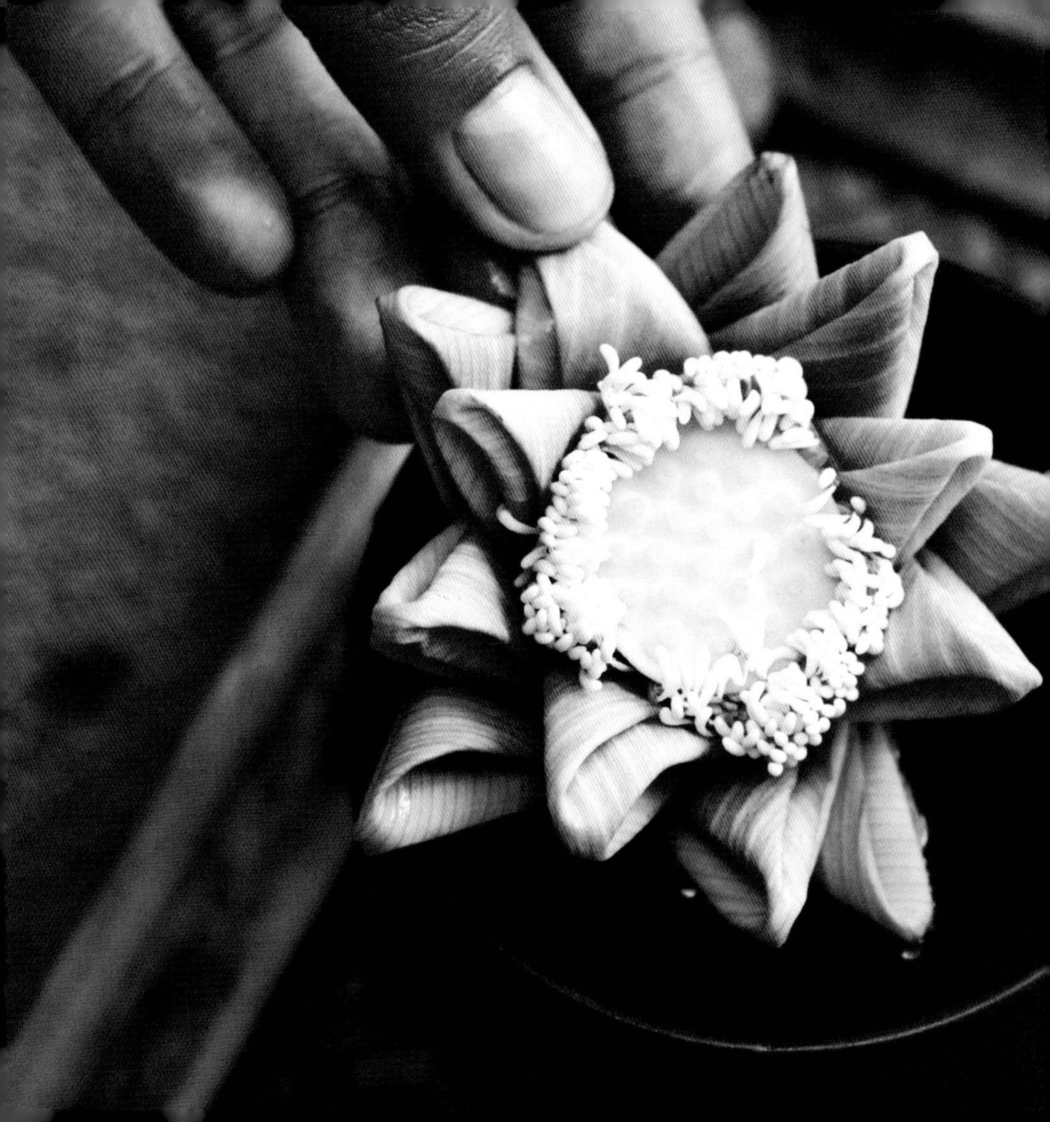

touches your heart

A sister is one
who reaches
for your hand,
and touches
your heart.

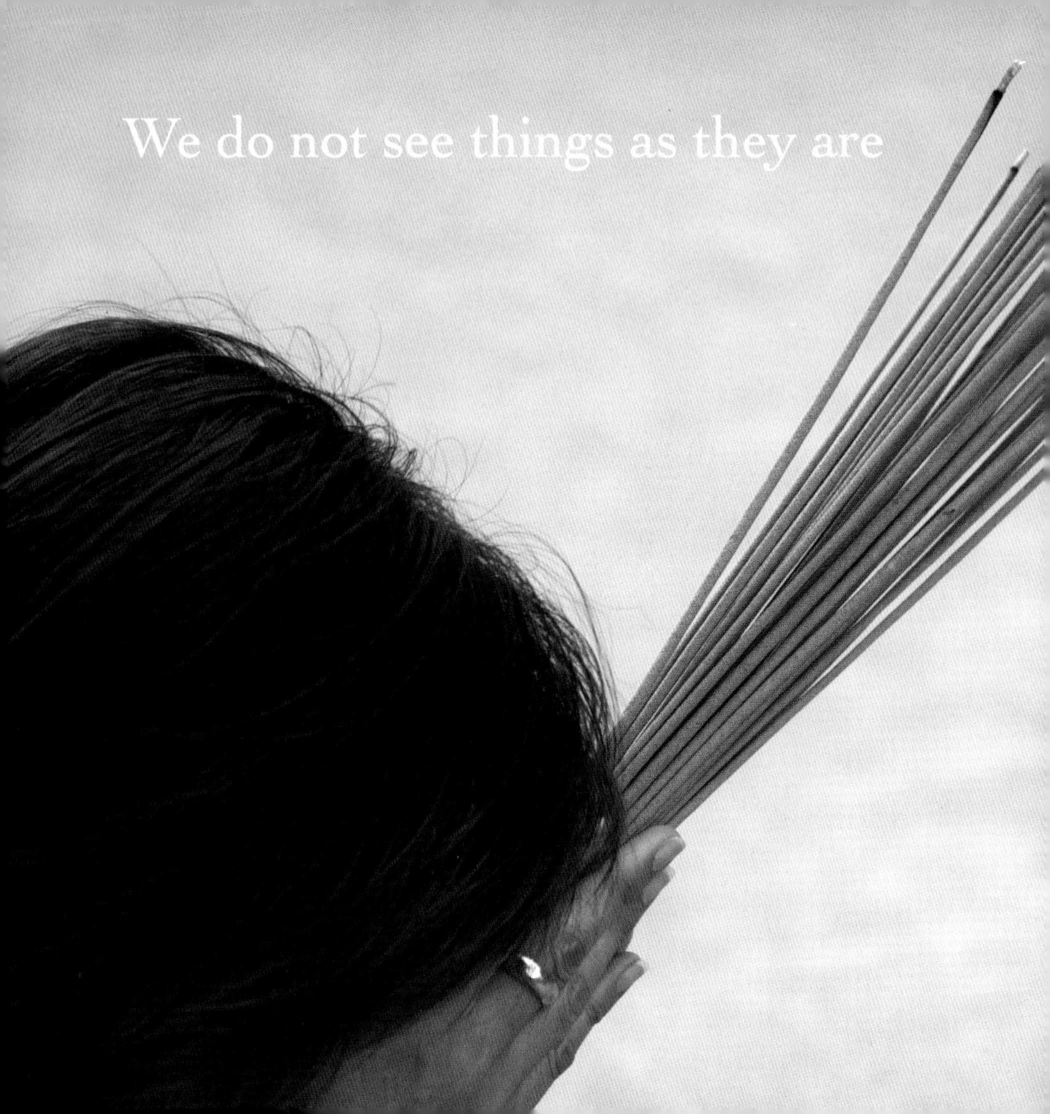
We do not see things as they are

we see them as we are.

The Talmud

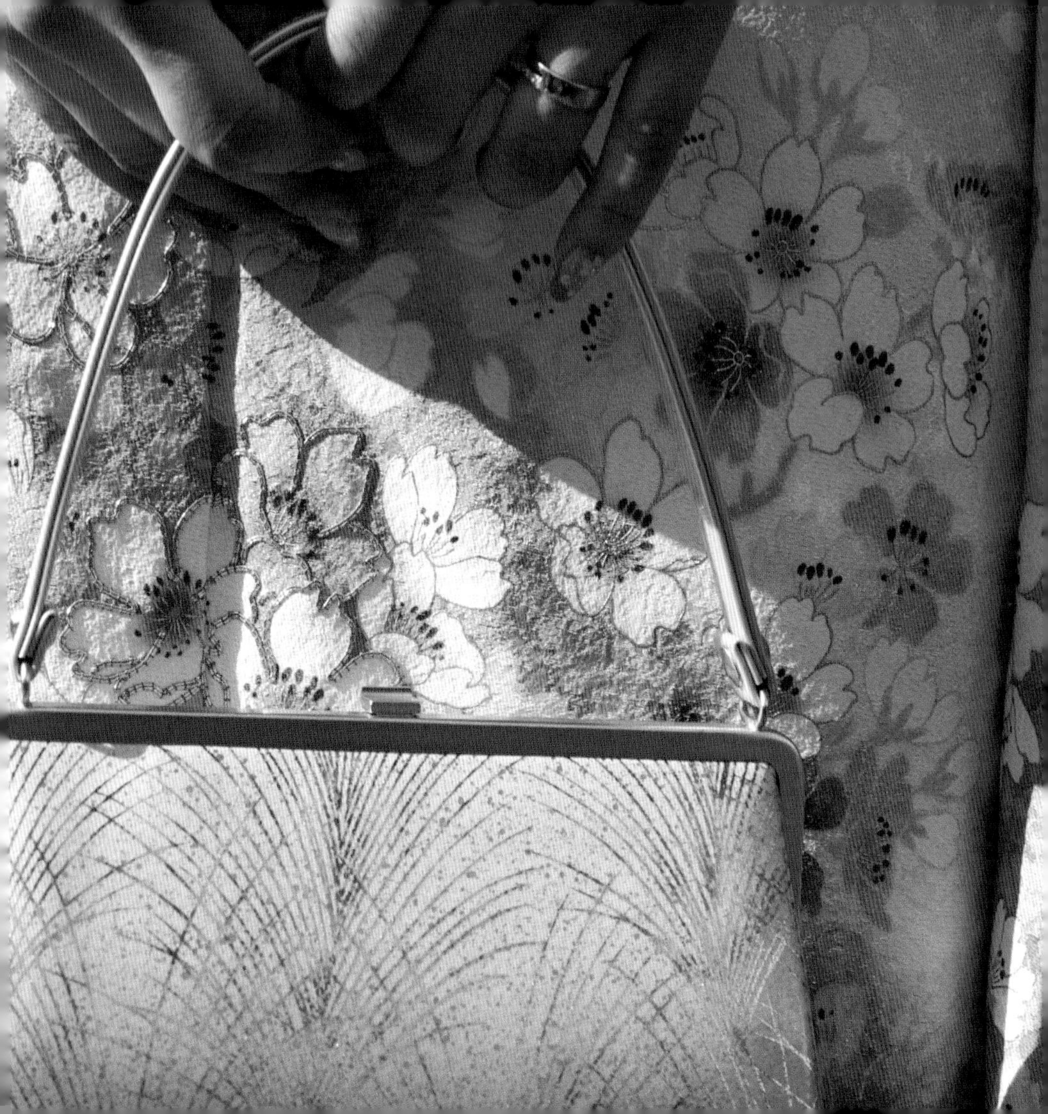

It is not flesh and blood, but

The heart

which makes us connected.

Johann Schiller

A sister

shares

childhood

memories

and

grown-up

dreams.

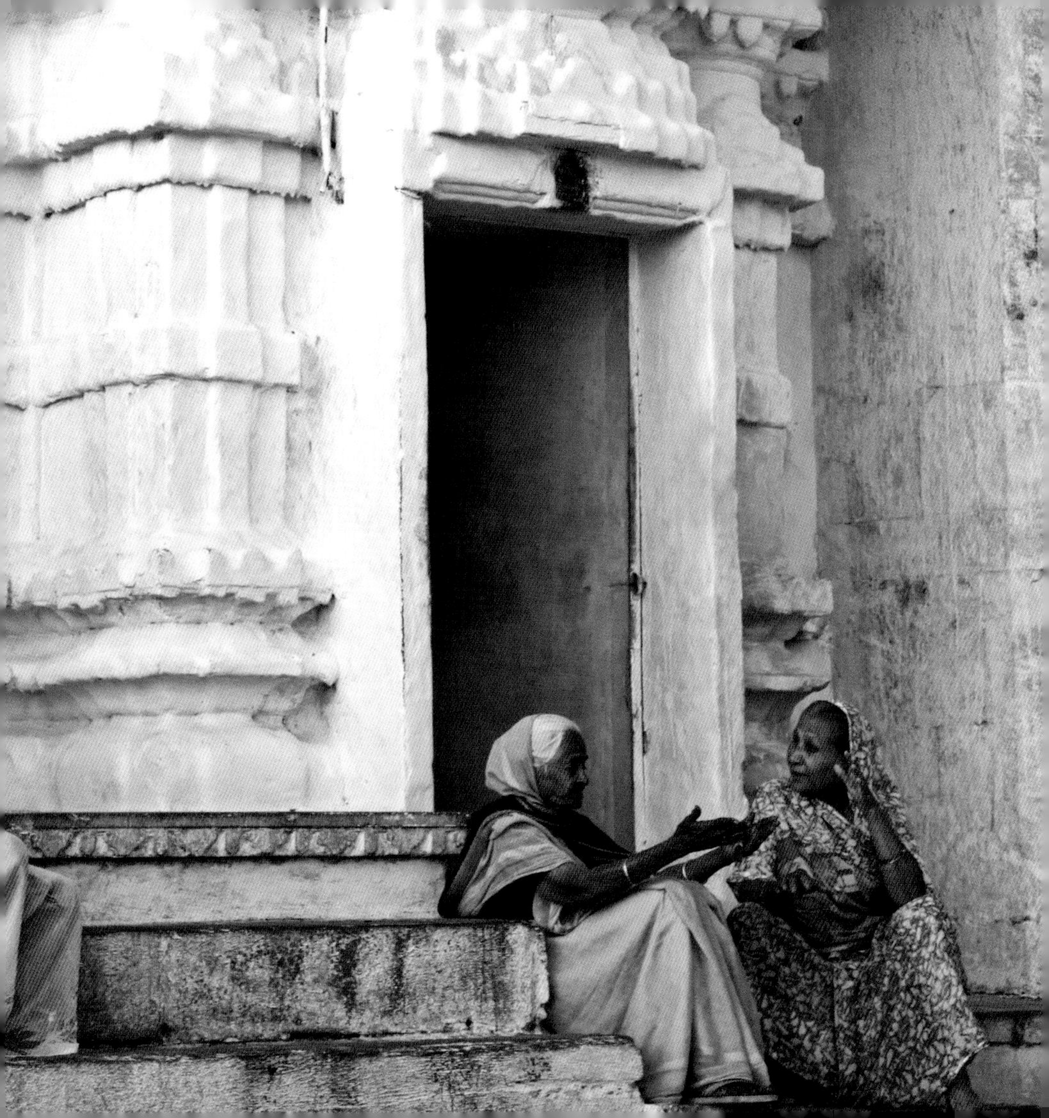

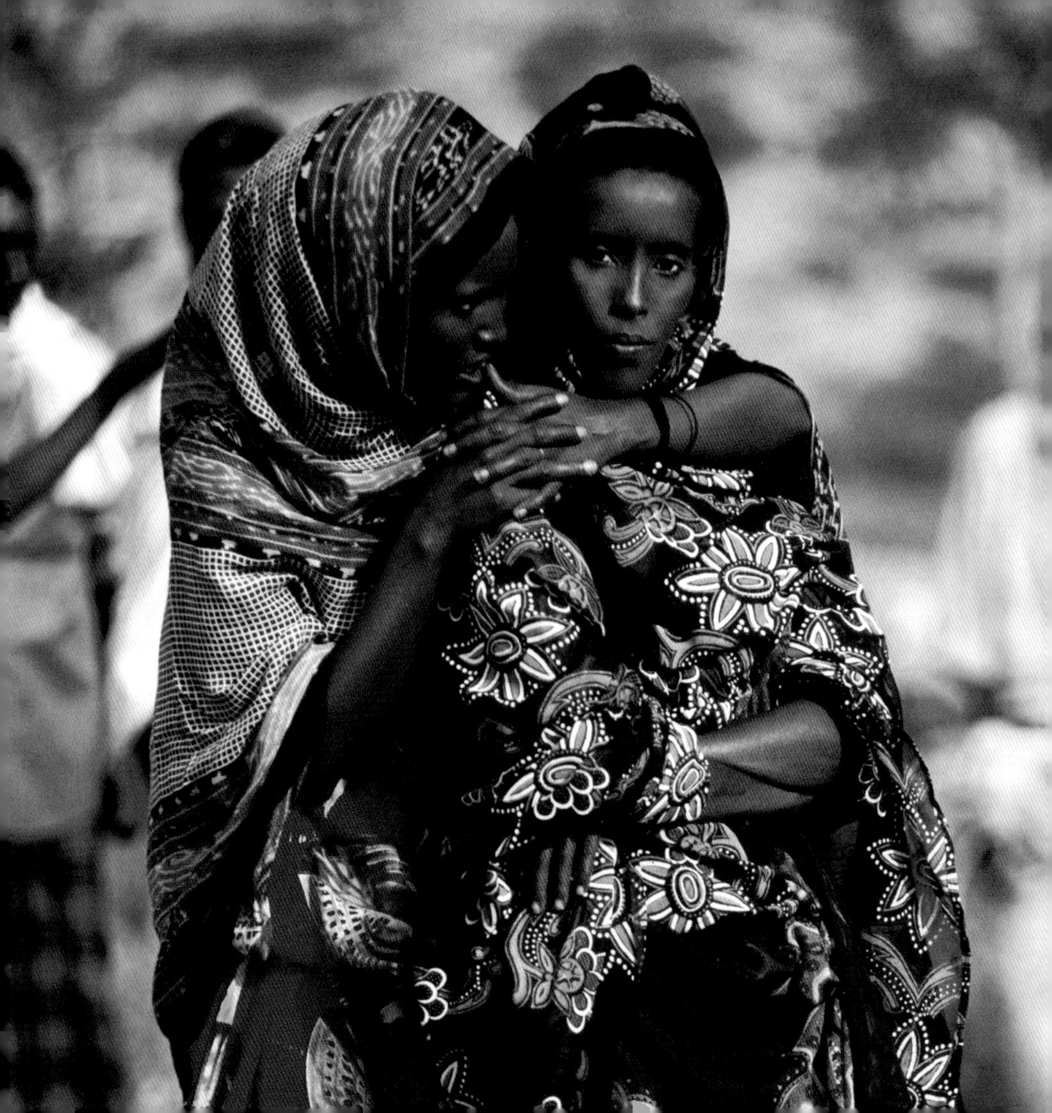

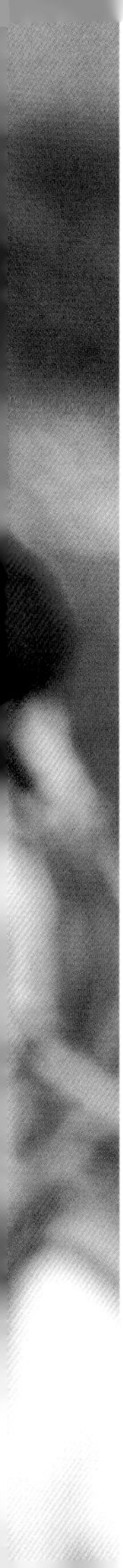

They are the family
we choose to surround us,
the sisters bound by love
instead of blood.
They know when we are lonely,
and appear without being called.
When we feel lost, they provide
a map to what comes next;
when we doubt
everything about ourselves,
they remind us of who we are.

Barbara Alpert

Sisters... they are the people
you share your secrets with,
cry with, laugh with,
and just be yourself with.
They don't judge you or make you change.
They accept you exactly as you are.
They look at you and they see a great person,
one they love spending time with.
You share something in common
and are tied together by memories,
tears, laughs and smiles.
Tied together by love for the other.

Sisterhood is heart, soul,
fun, laughter, tears, love and life.

you are a precious

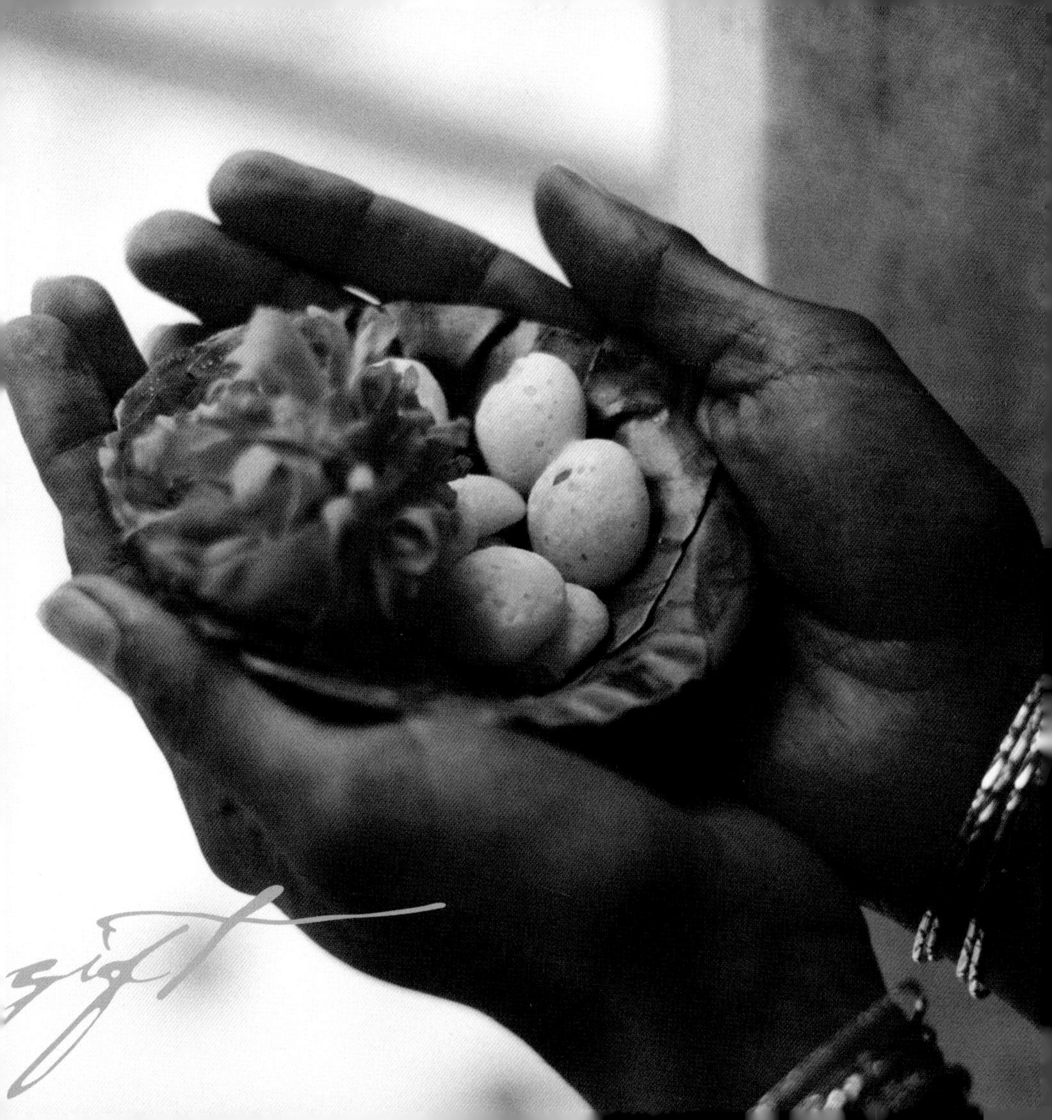

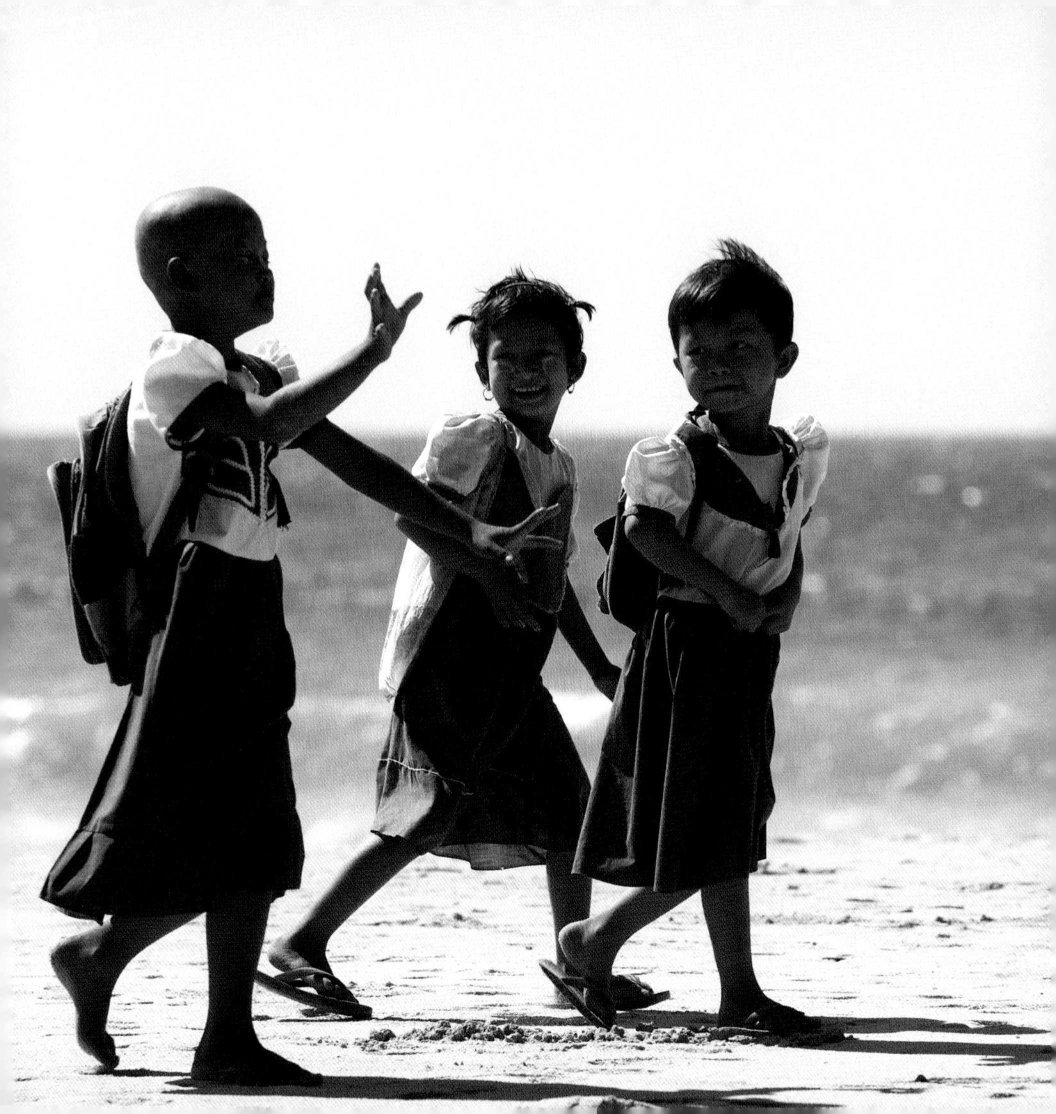

a sister is

a little bit of childhood
that can never be lost.

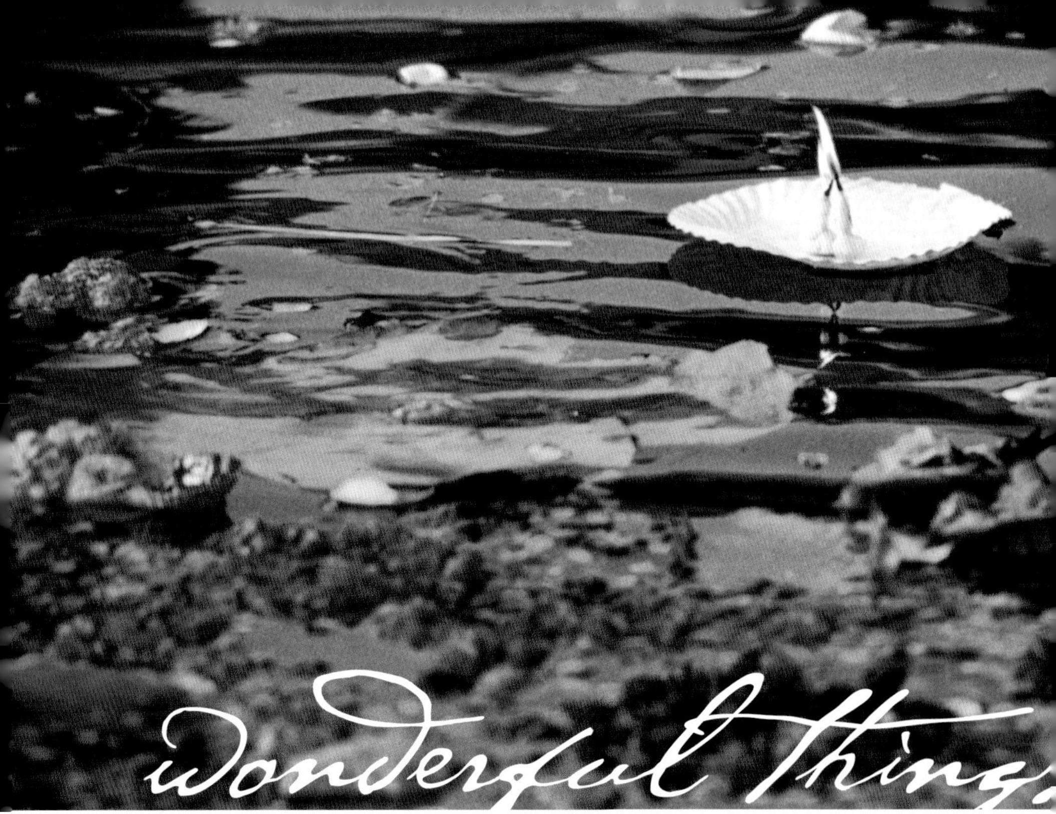
wonderful thing

Give of yourself as angels do and

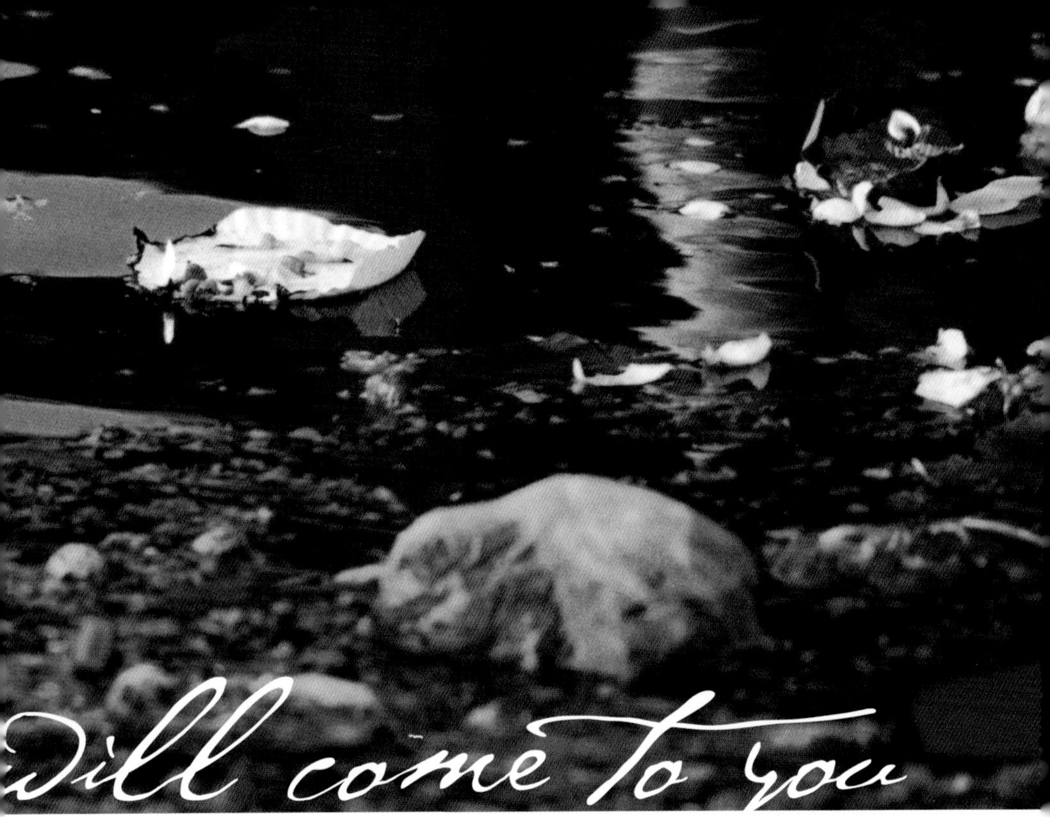
ill come to you

wonderful things will come to you.

Ramadan

I sought my soul,
but my soul I could not see.
I sought my faith,
but my faith eluded me.
I sought my sister
and I found all three.

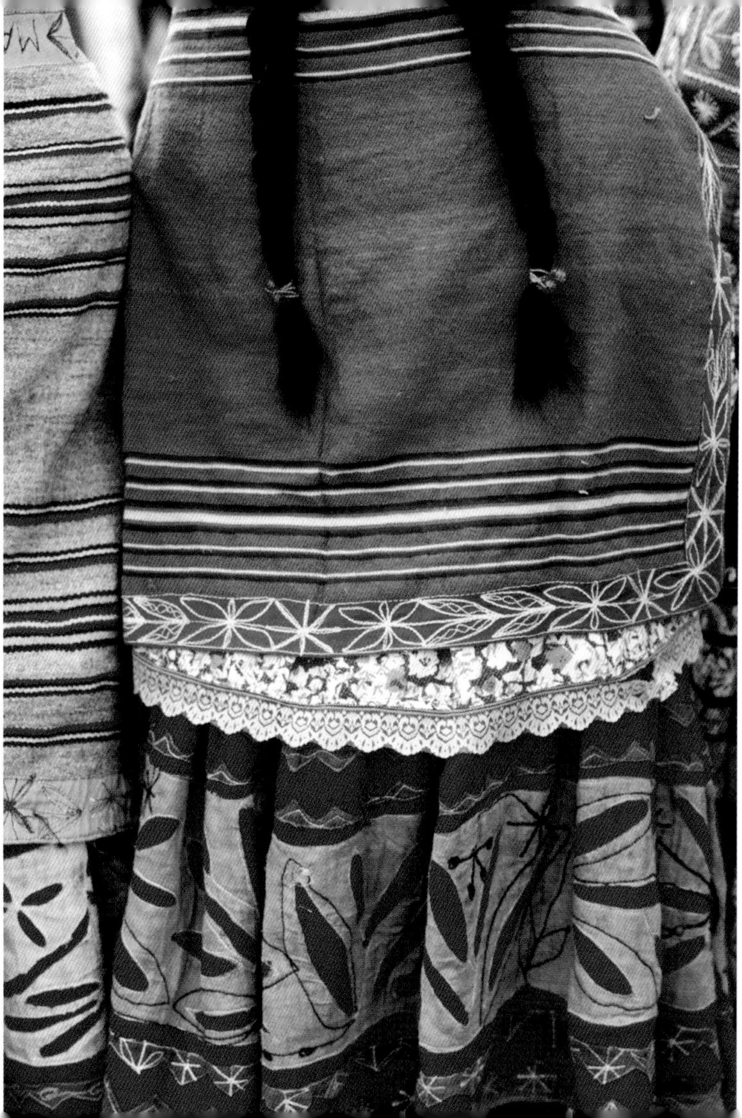

gentle

loving

reliable

faithful

tender

honourable

responsible

loyal

inspiring

kind-hearted

compassionate

warm

feeling

affectionate

good

sister

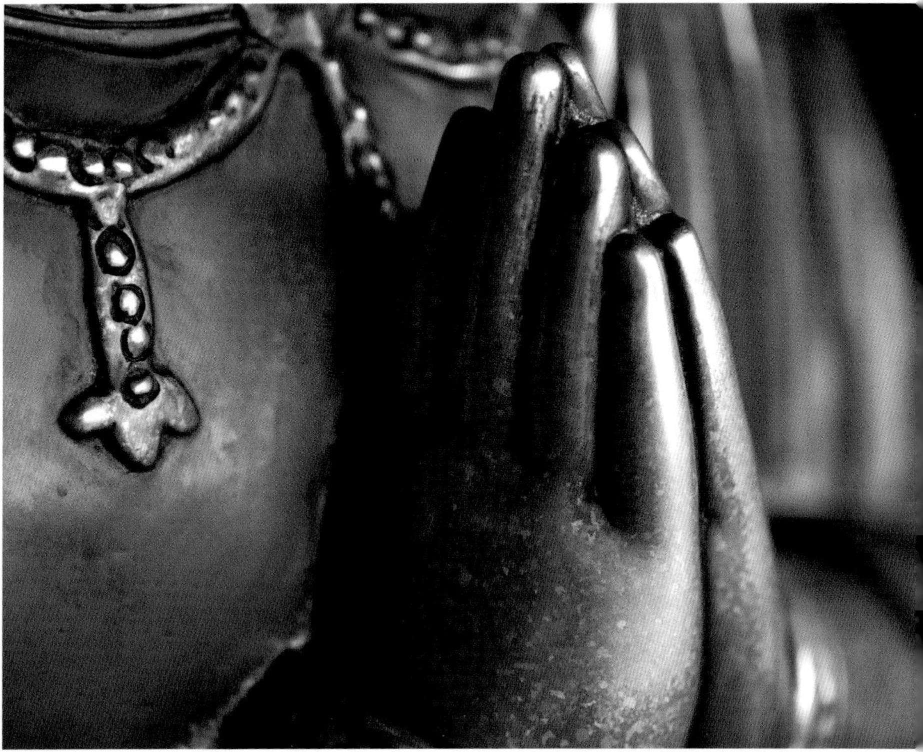

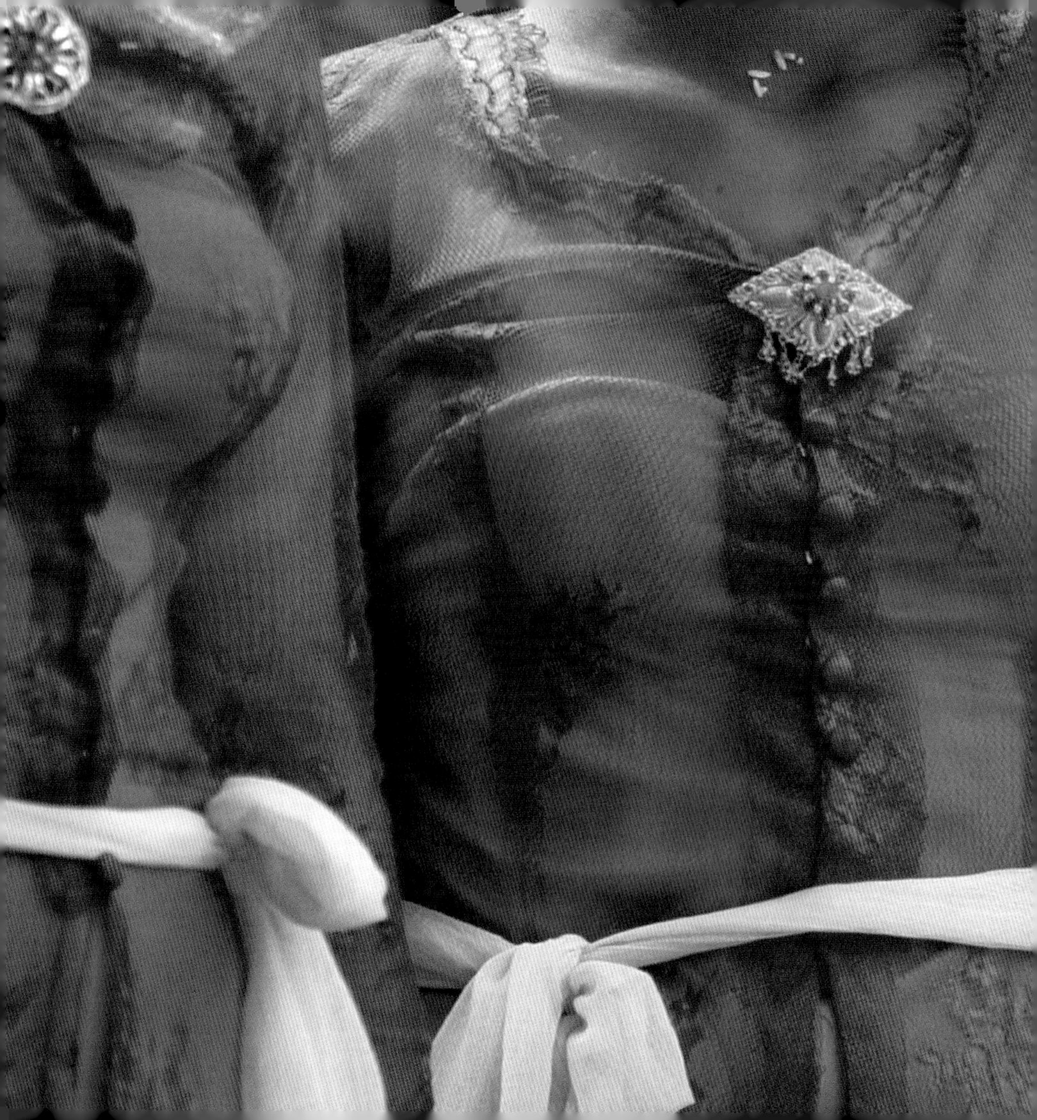

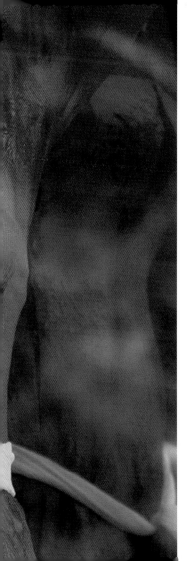

All for one
and one for all
My sister
and my friend
What fun we have
The time we share
Sisters 'til the end.

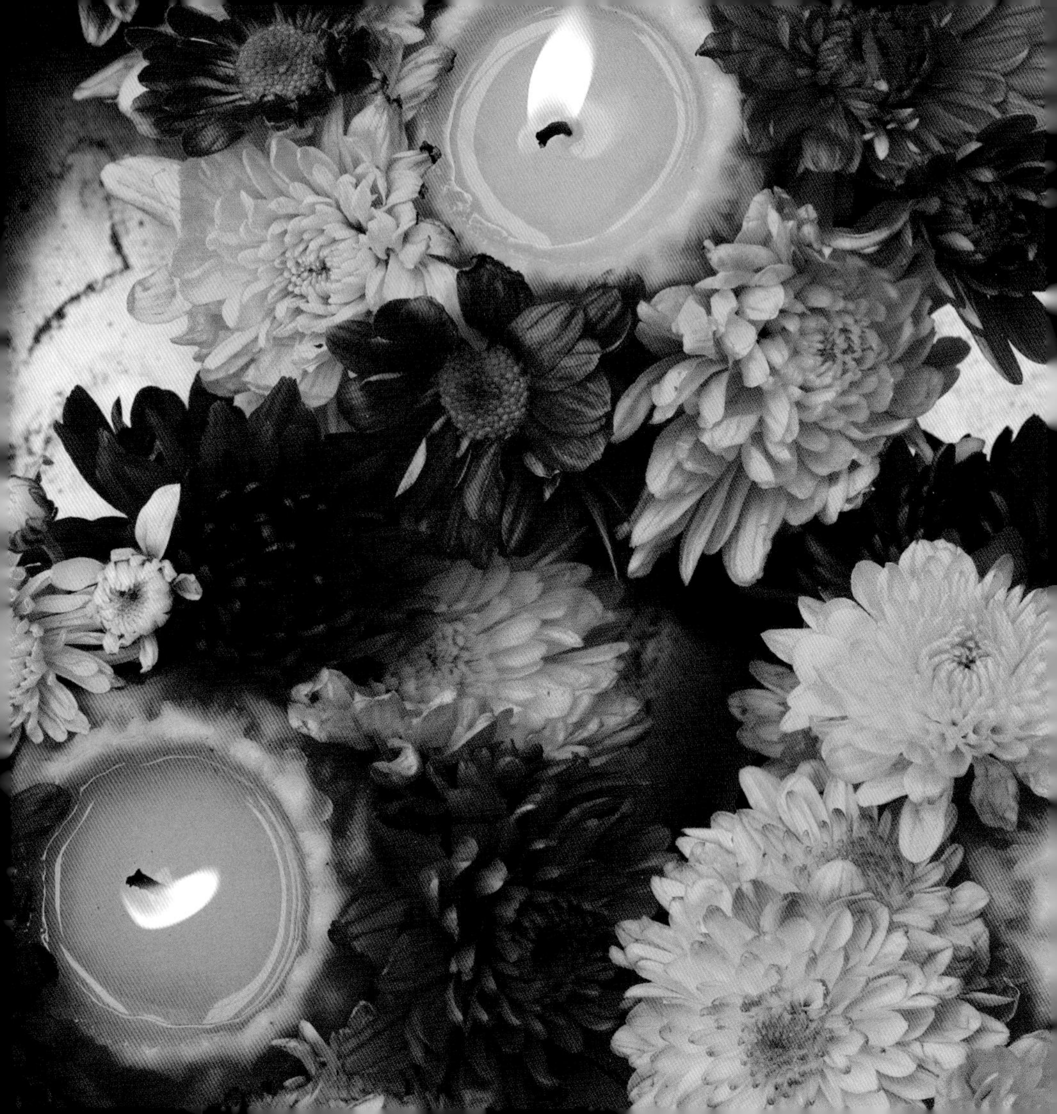

There are two ways
to spread the light.
Be the candle,
or the mirror
that reflects it.

Edith Wharton

Stories of

the heart

are what live
in the memory.

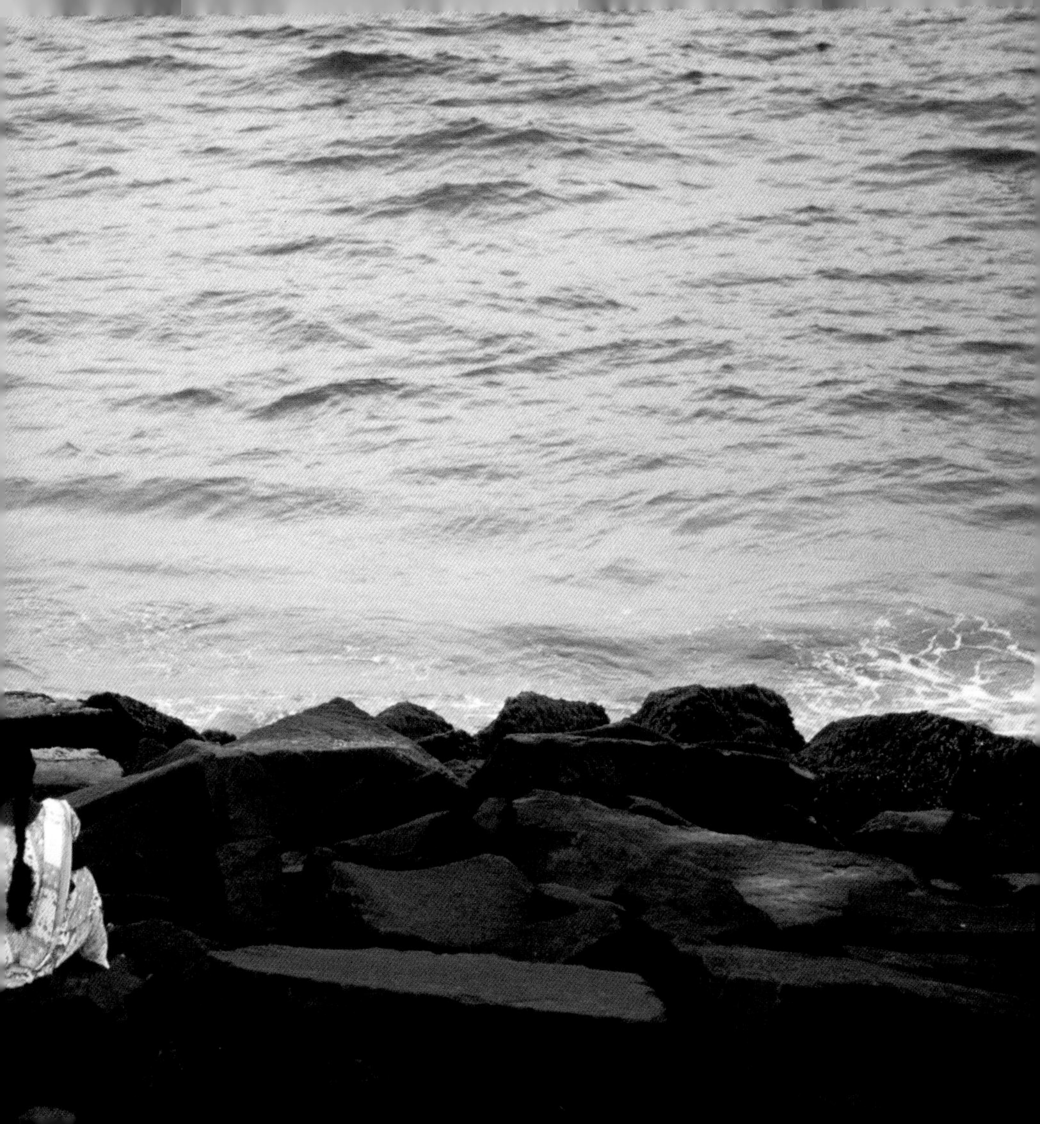

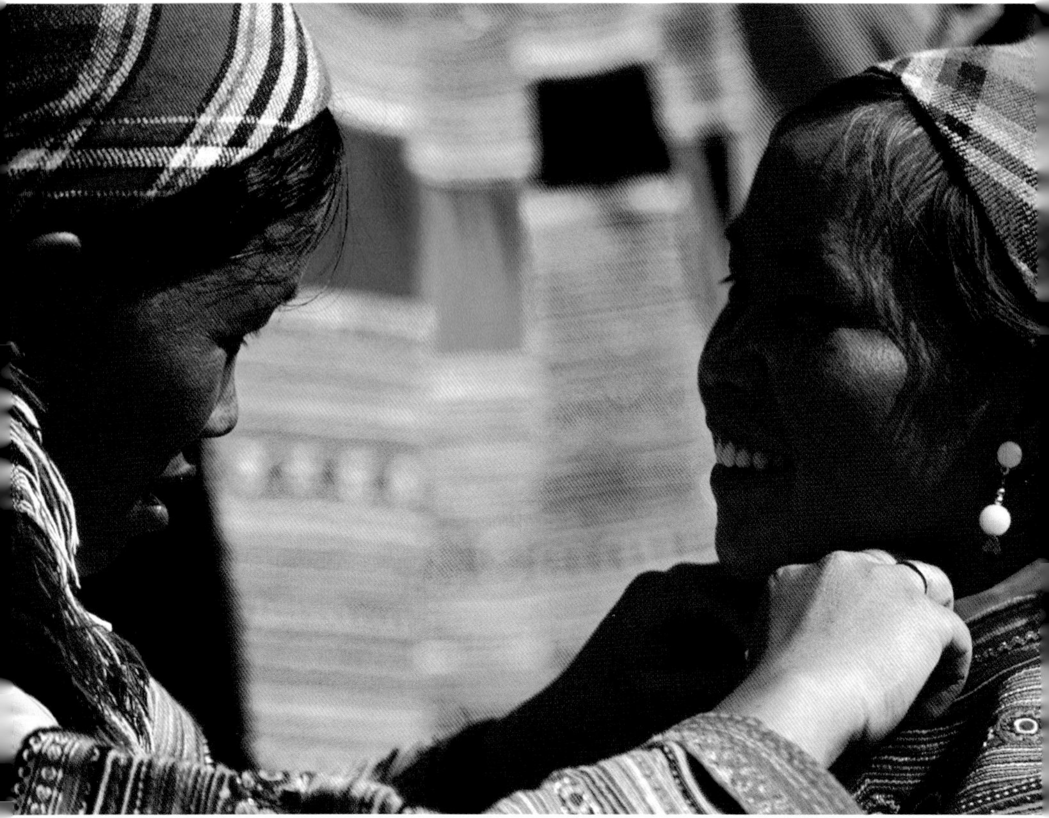

She is your mirror,
shining back at you
with a world of possibilities.
She is your witness,
who sees you at your worst and best,
and loves you anyway.
She is your partner in crime,
your midnight companion,
someone who knows
when you are smiling,
even in the dark.

Barbara Alpert

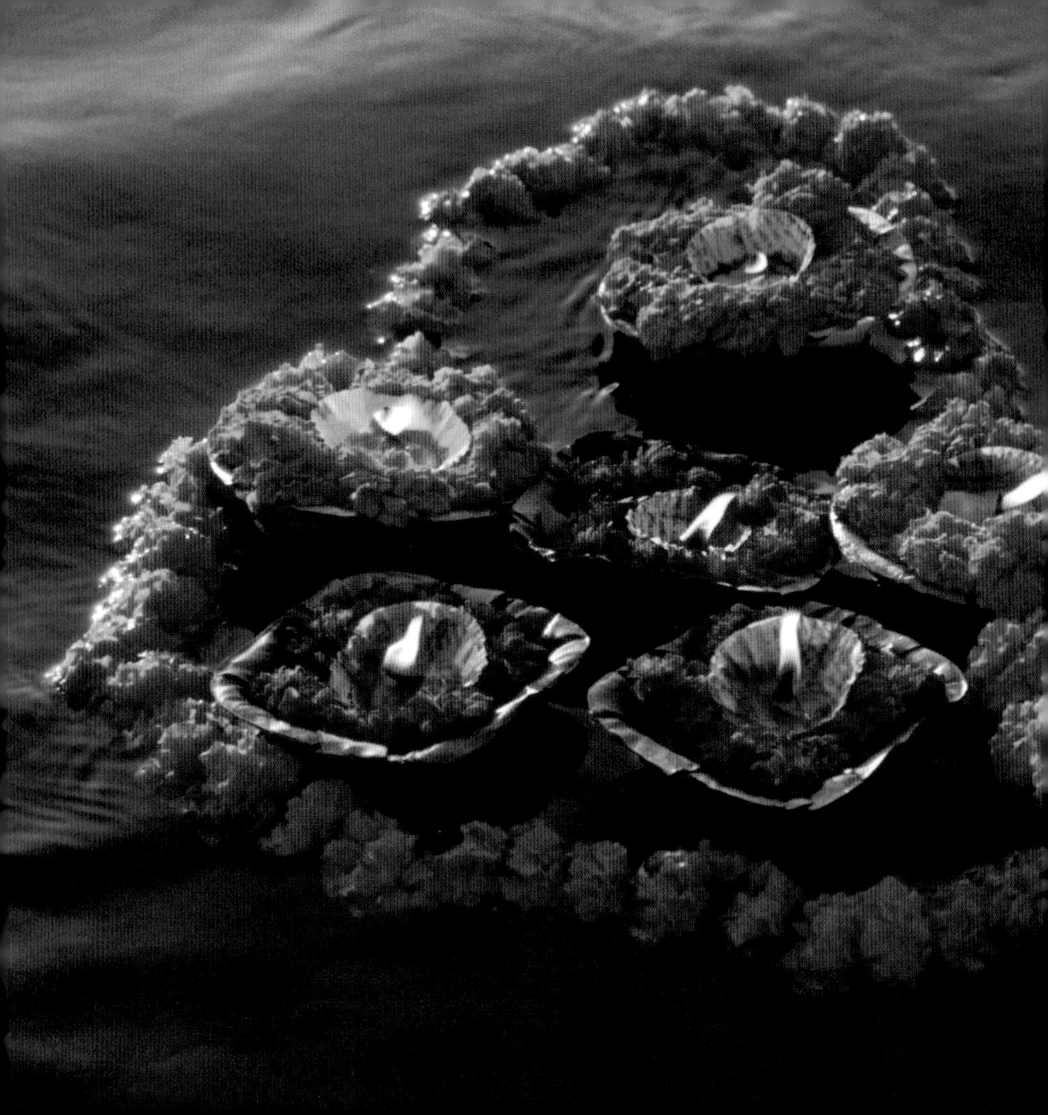

The best
thing
to give
your friend
is your
heart.

Francis Maitland Balfour

Let there be laughter

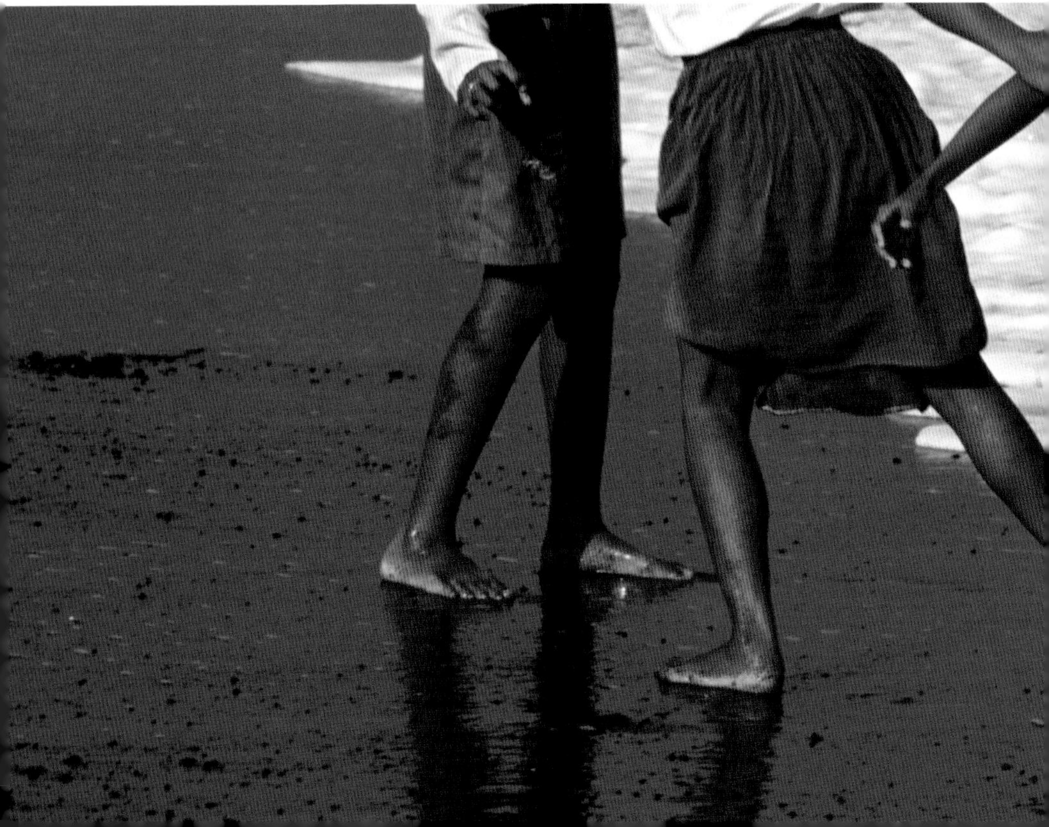

and the sharing of pleasures.

Kahlil Gibran

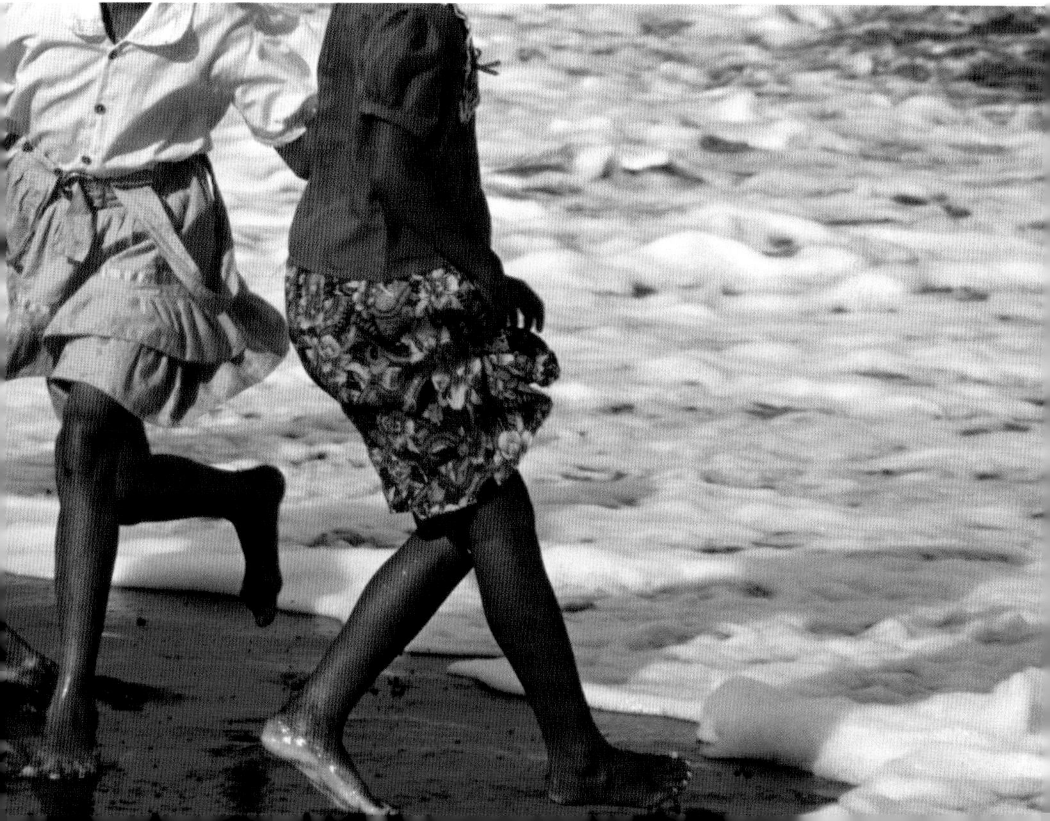

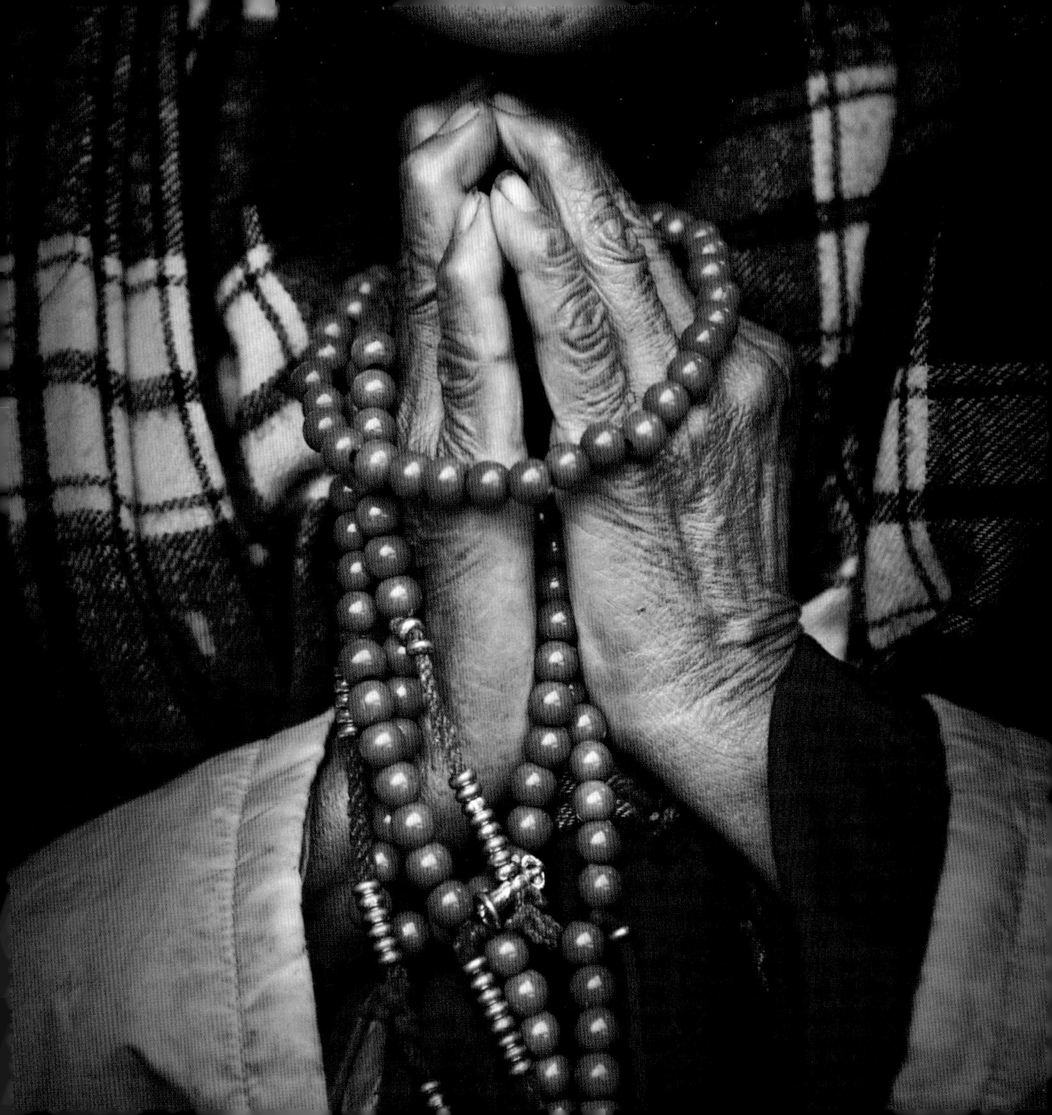

If the essence of my being
has caused a smile
to have appeared
upon your face,
or a touch of joy
within your heart,
then in living
I have made my mark.

Thomas L Odem Jr

You are a part
of all
you have met.

Alfred Lord Tennyson

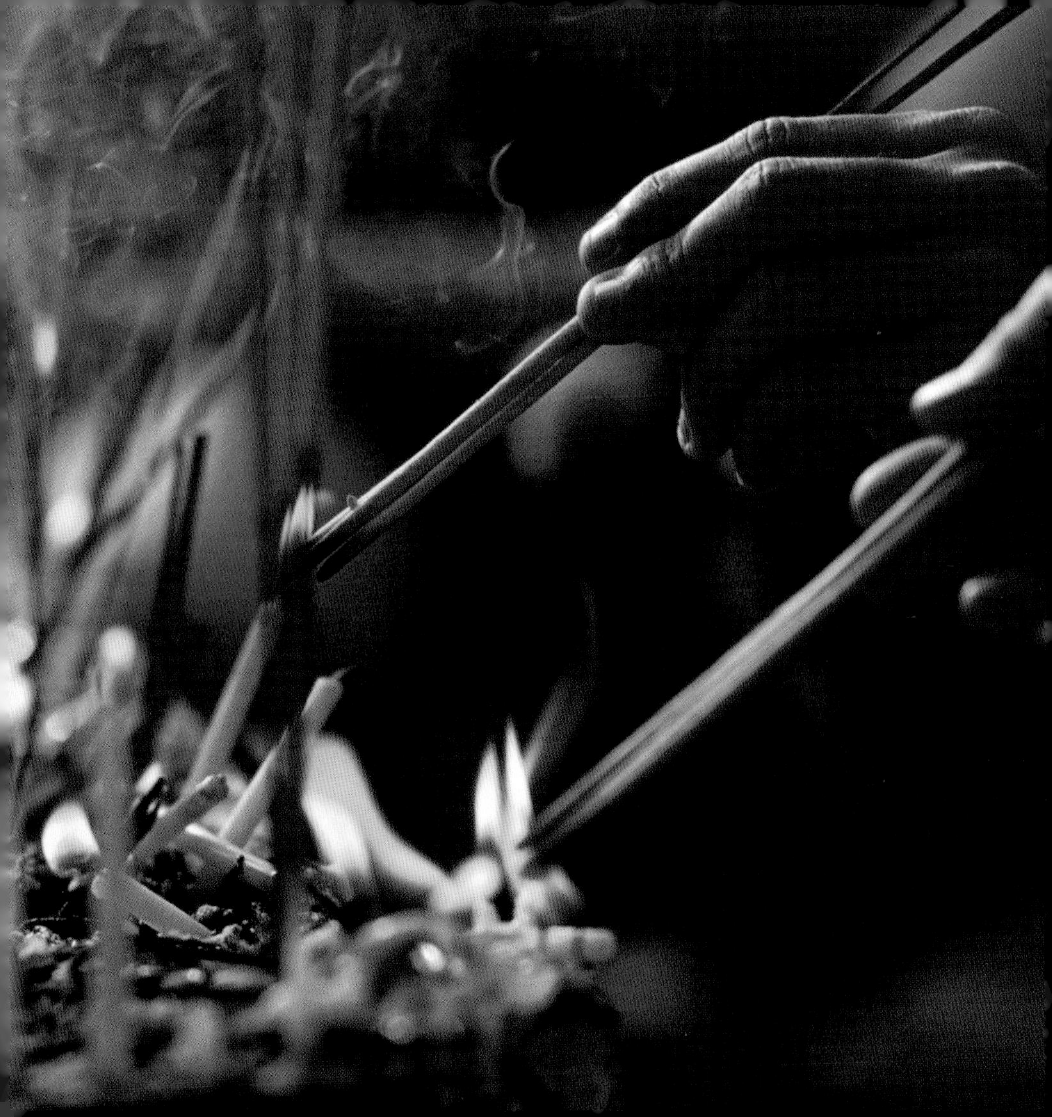

I never came to you and went away
without some new enrichment of the heart;
more faith and less of doubt,
more courage in the days ahead.
And often in coming to you,
I went away comforted indeed.
How can I find the shining word,
the glowing phrase that tells
all that your love has meant to me.
There is no word, no phrase for you
on whom I so depend.
All I can say is this:

precious friend

Bless you, my precious friend.

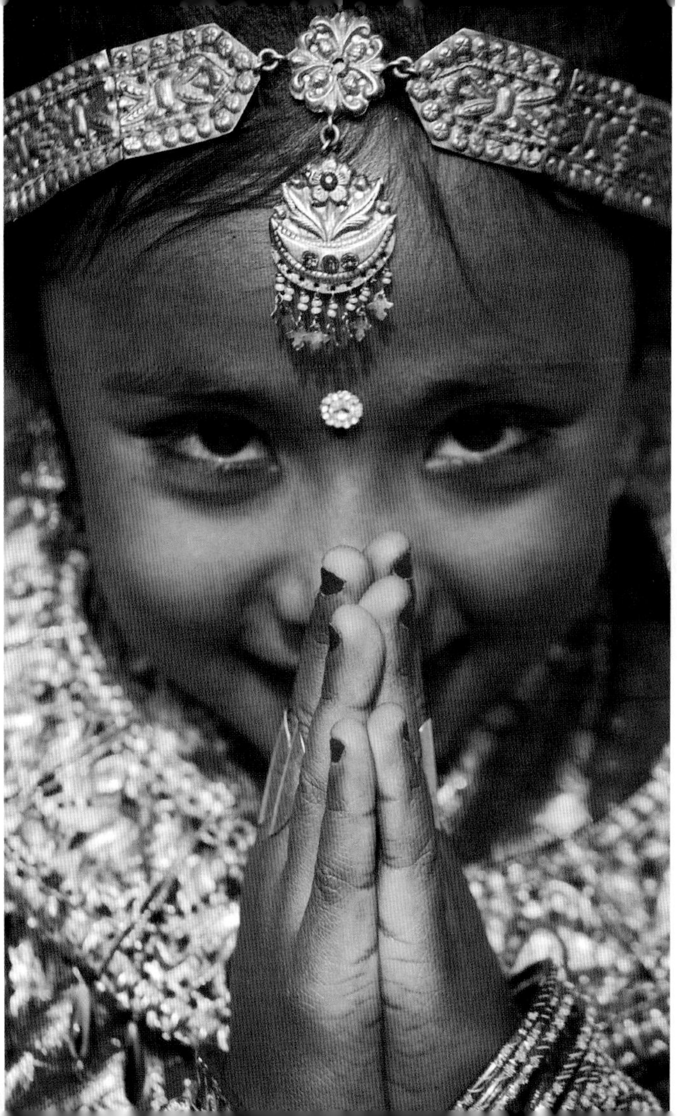

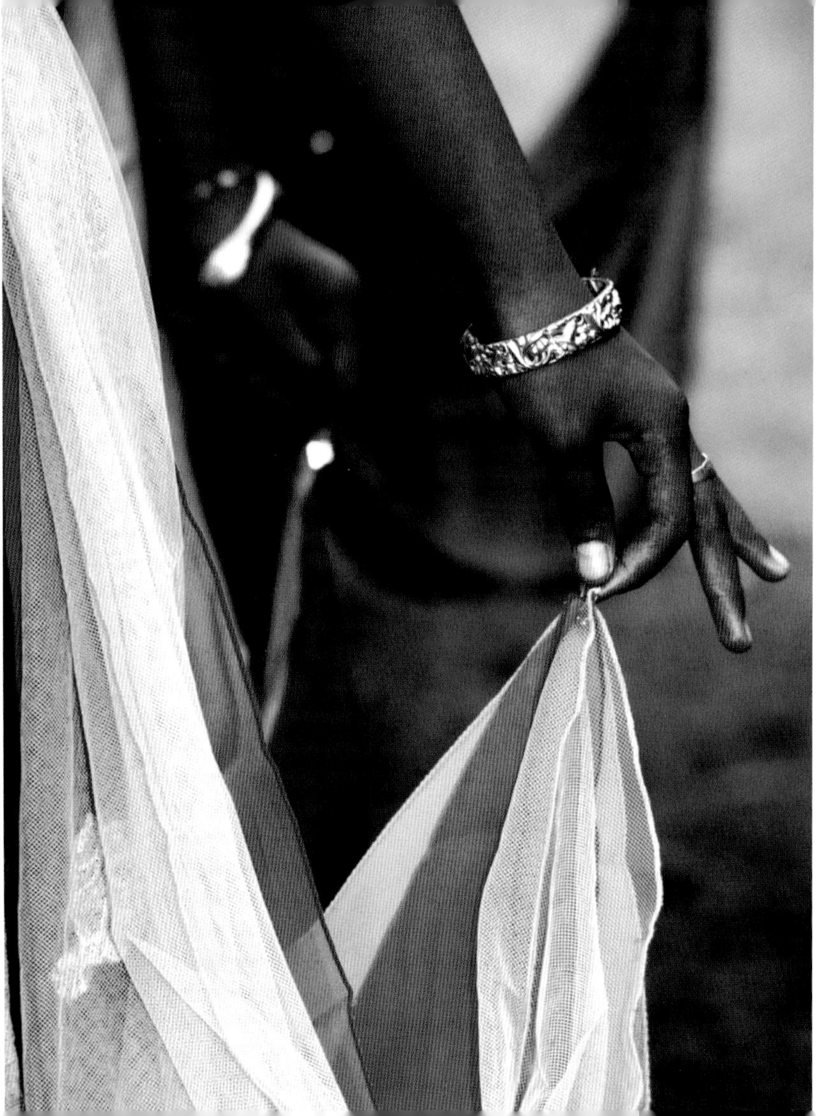

dear

devoted

patient

empathetic

uplifting

interconnected

passionate

thoughtful

committed

friendly

comforting

sensitive

considerate

accommodating

lovely

sister

You
deserve
to be
happy.

You
deserve
delight.

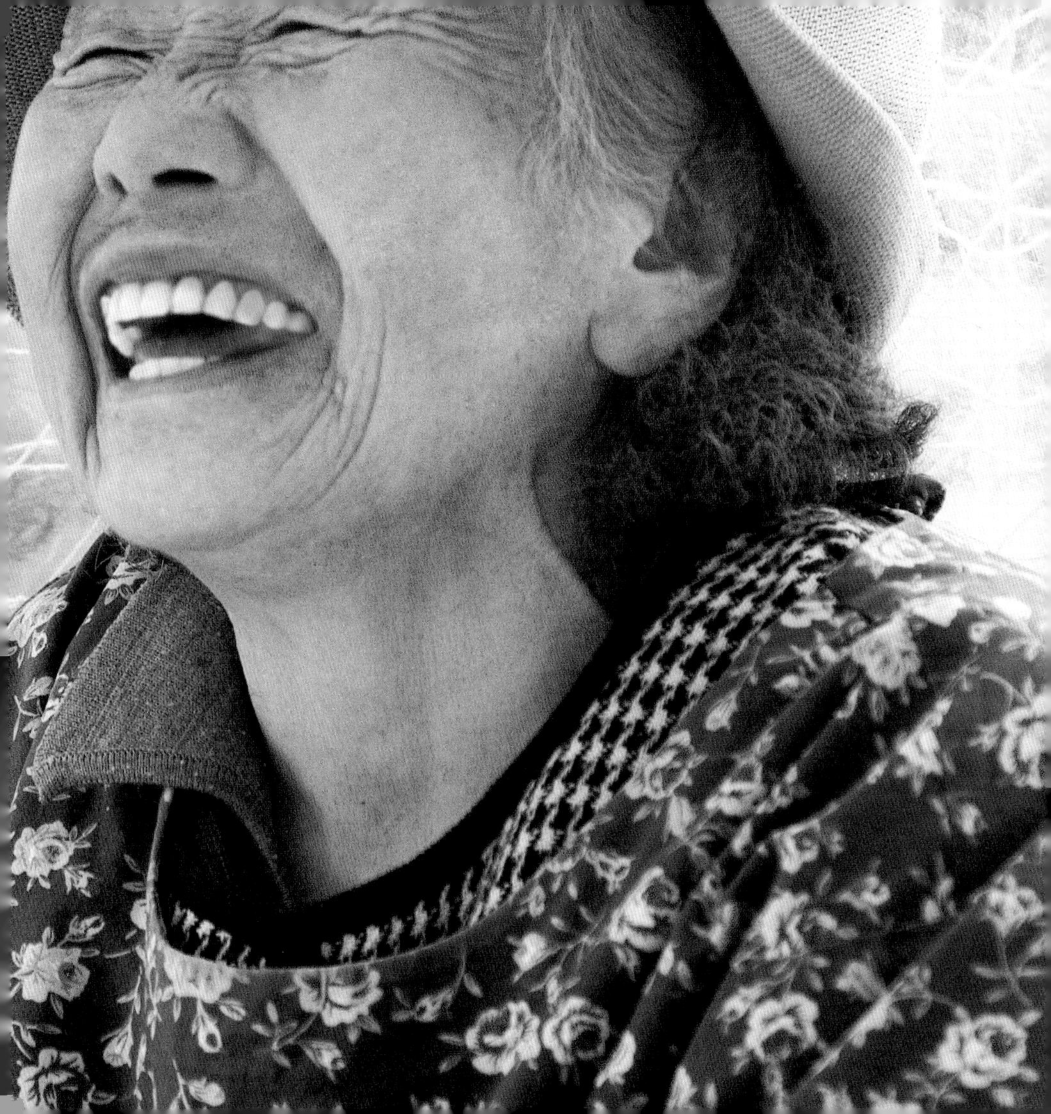

May our paths
always
lead back to

each other.

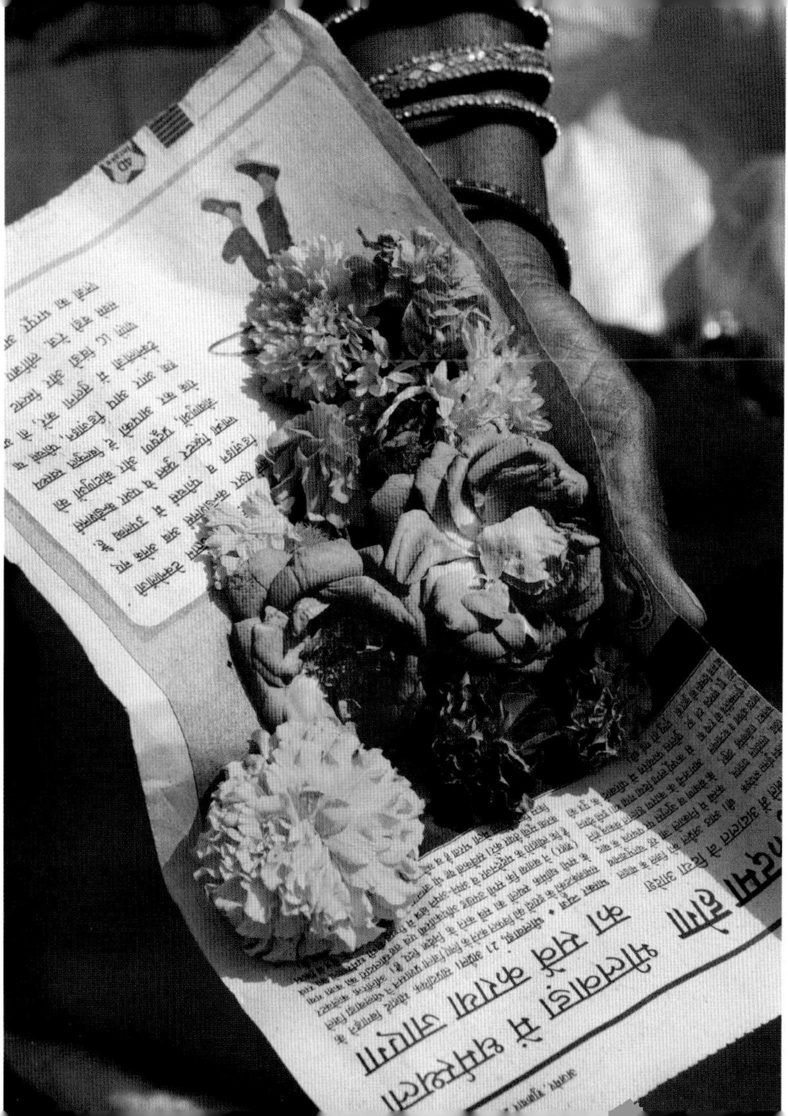

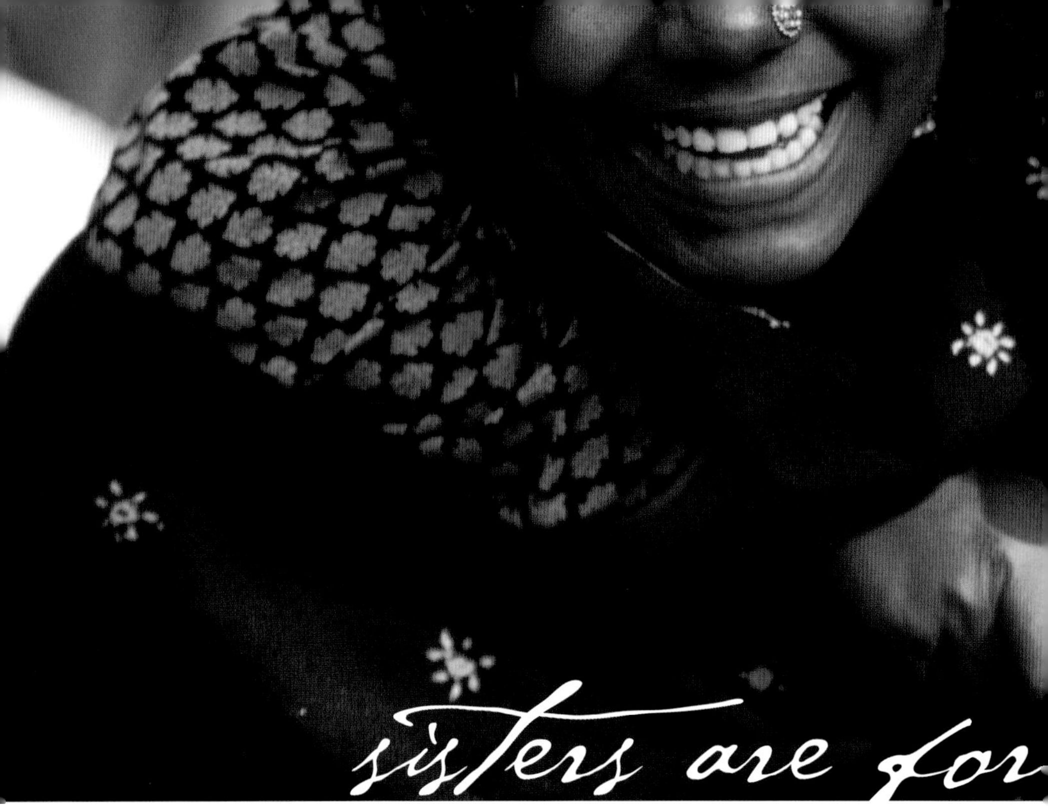
sisters are for

Sisters are for sharing laughter

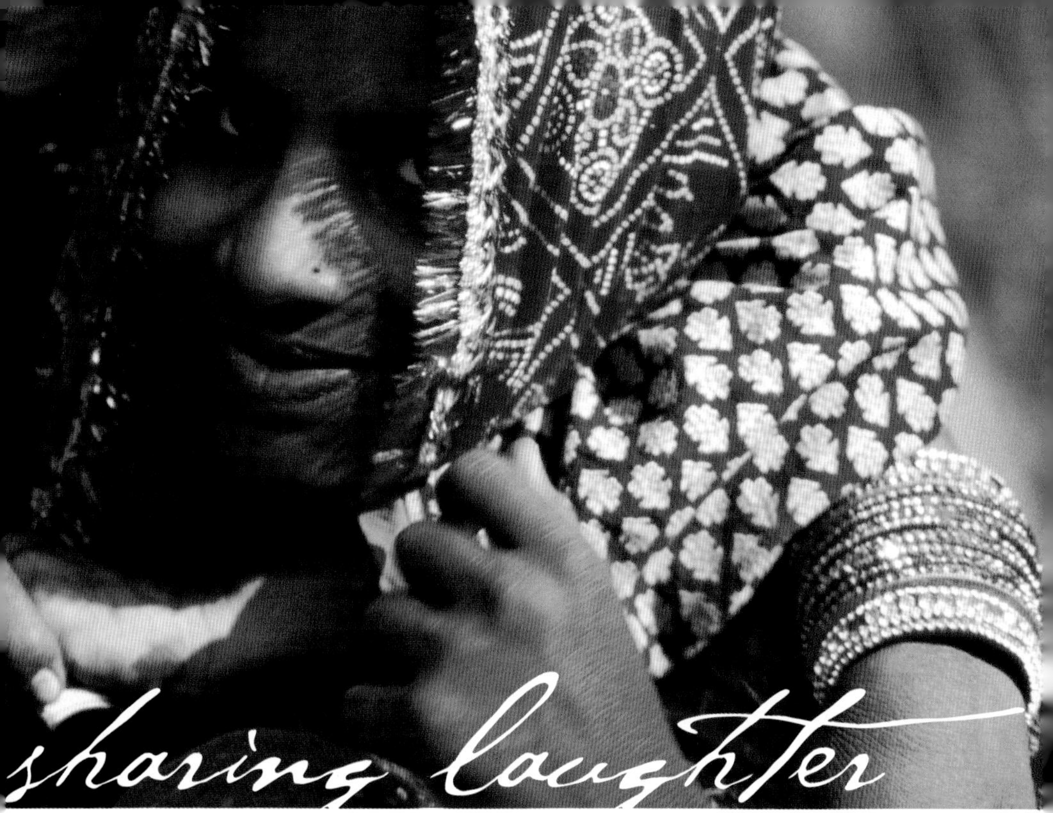
sharing laughter

and wiping away tears.

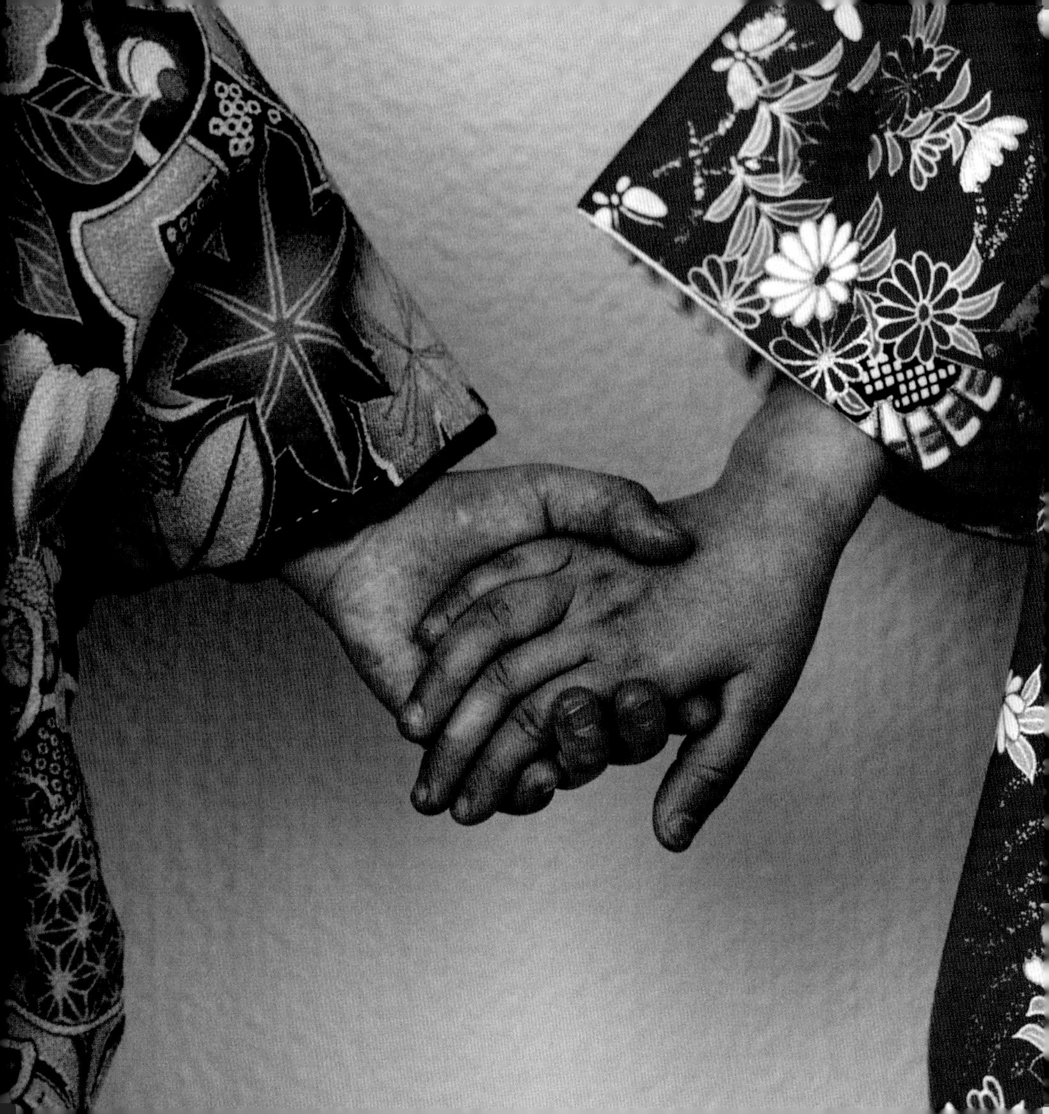

Looking back on all that's happened,

growing up, growing together...

there were times when we dreamed together,
when we laughed and cried together.
As I look back on those days,
I realise how much I truly love you.

The past may be gone forever
and whatever the future holds,
our todays make the memories of tomorrow.

So, my lifetime friend,
it is with all my heart I send you my love,
hoping you will always carry my smile with you,
for all we have meant to each other
and for whatever the future may hold.

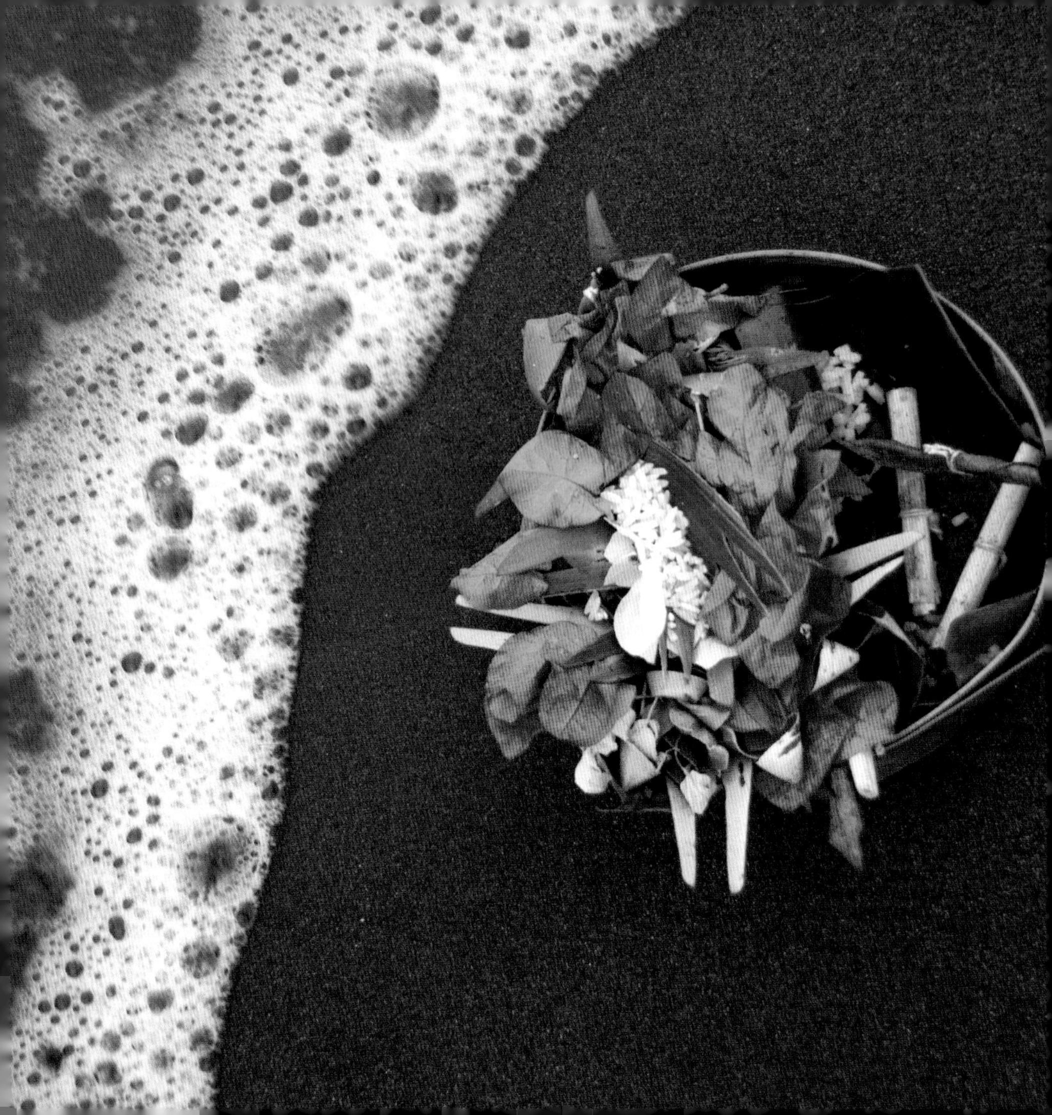

You are
and always
will be
here.

I'll lift you,
and you lift me,
and we will both ascend

Together.

John Greenleaf Whittier

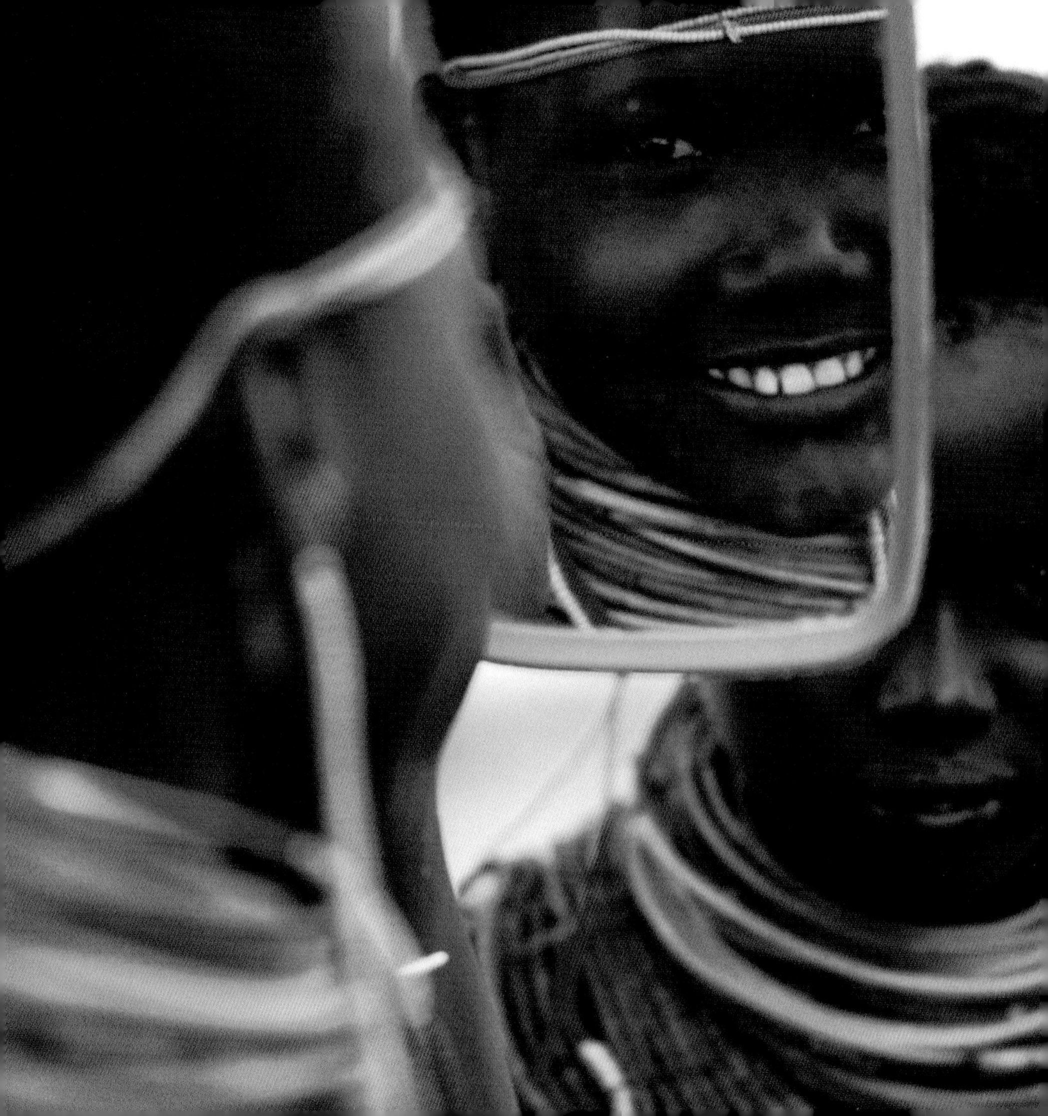

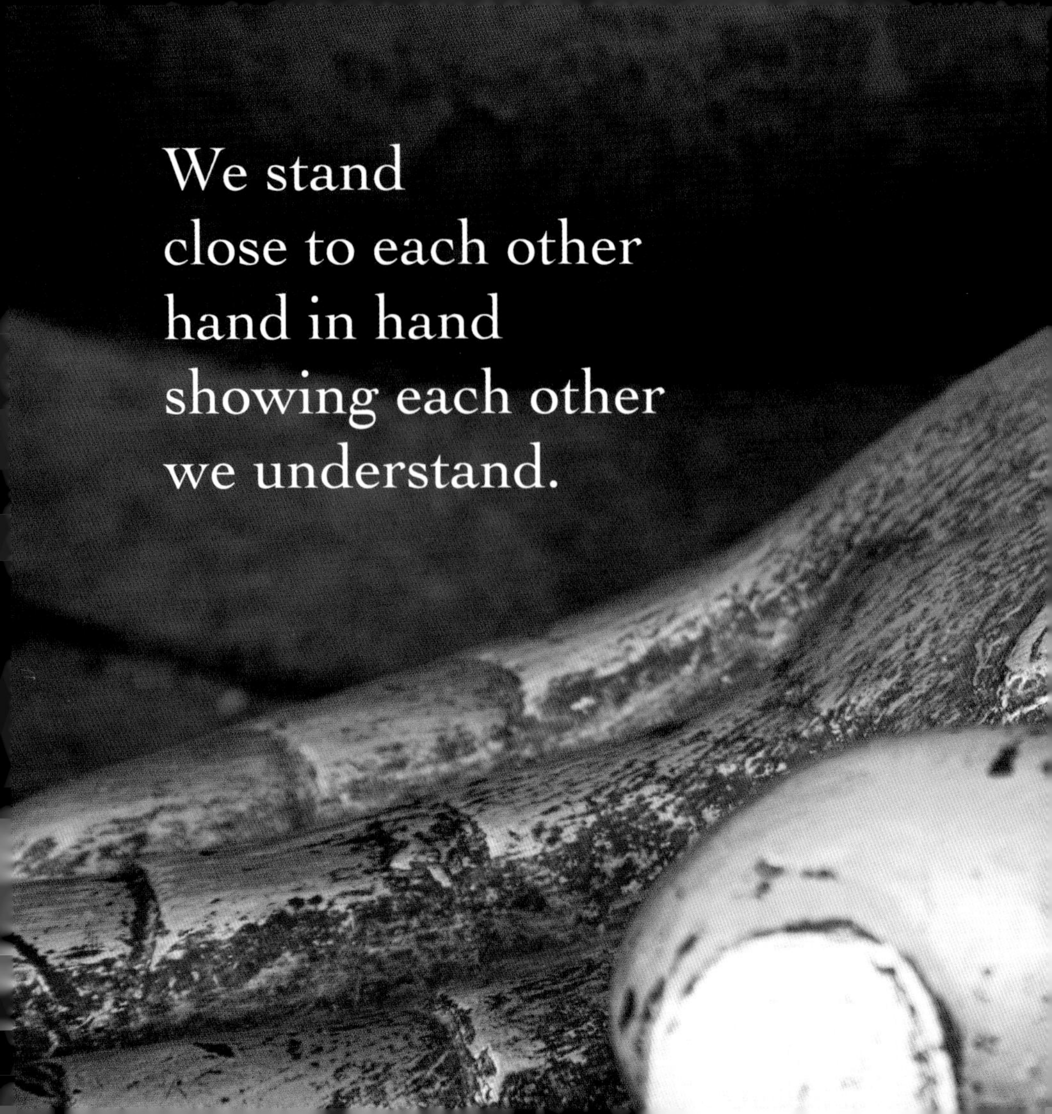

We stand
close to each other
hand in hand
showing each other
we understand.

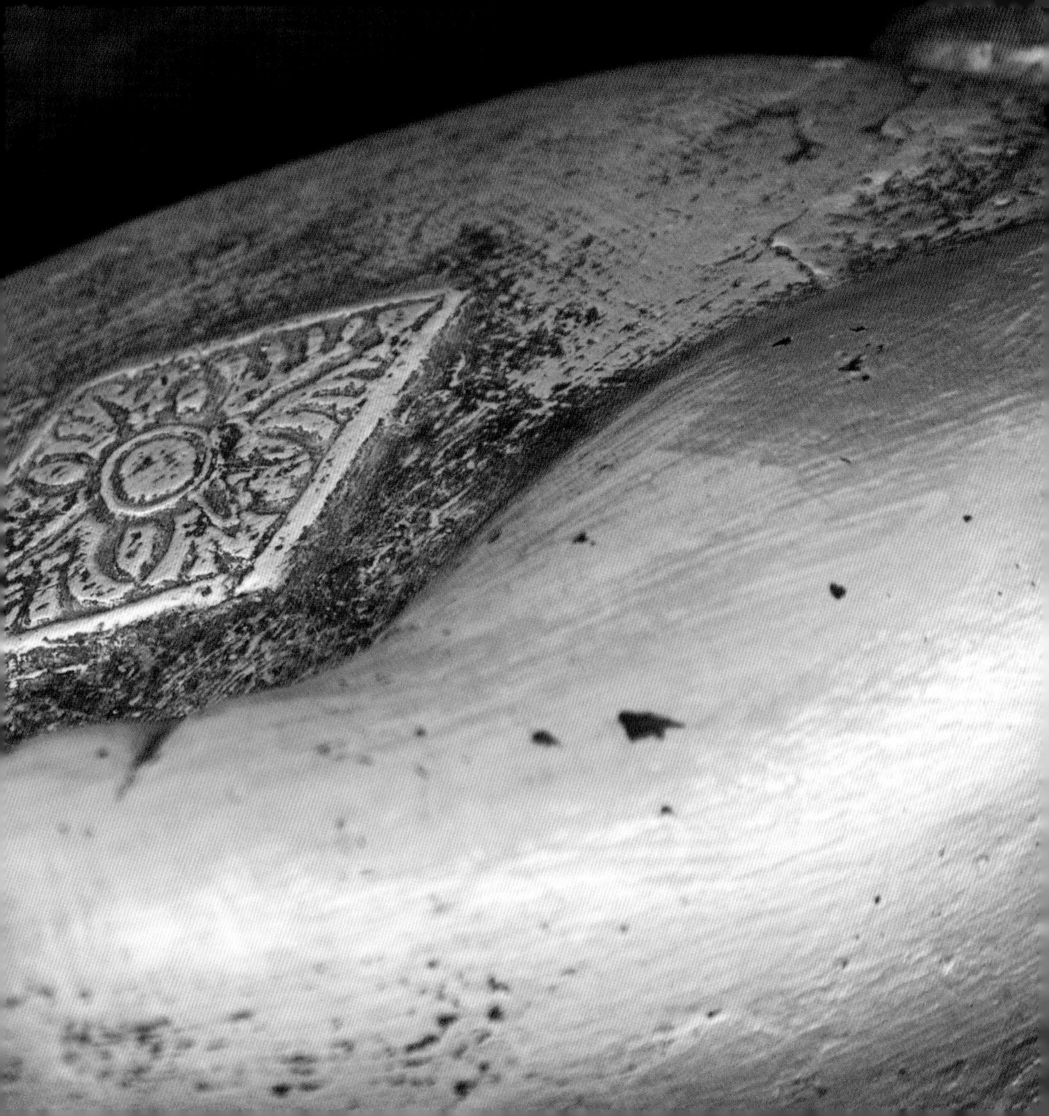

A true
sister
is a
friend

who

listens

with her

heart.

There is nothing more comforting

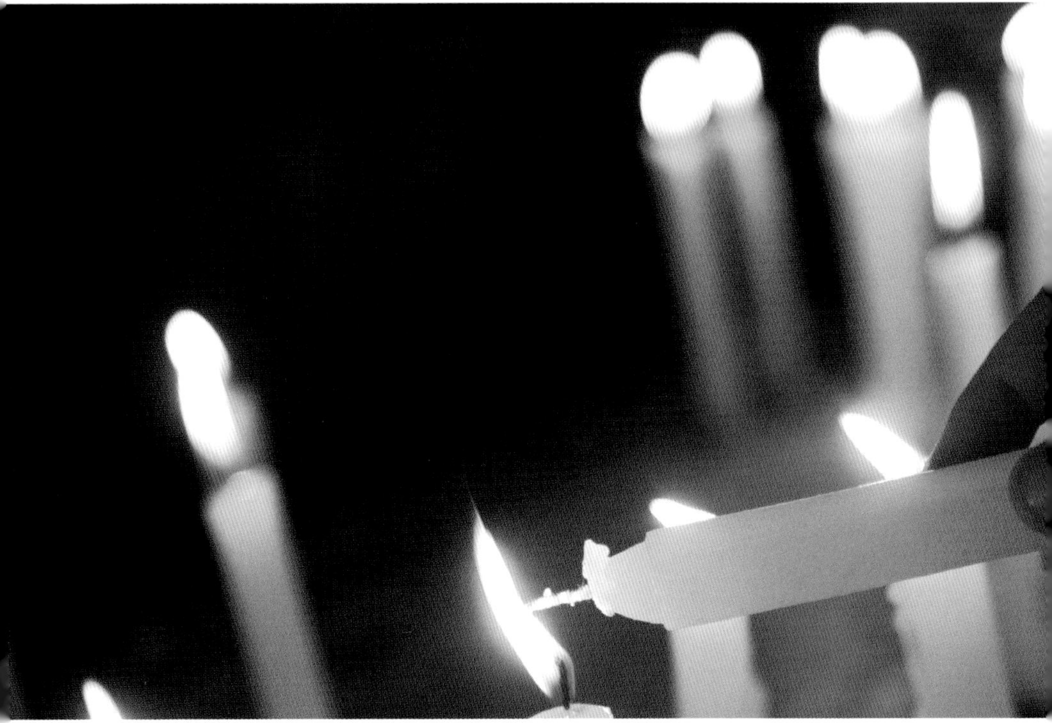

han knowing

you are near the ones you love.

Sisters
don't
need
words.

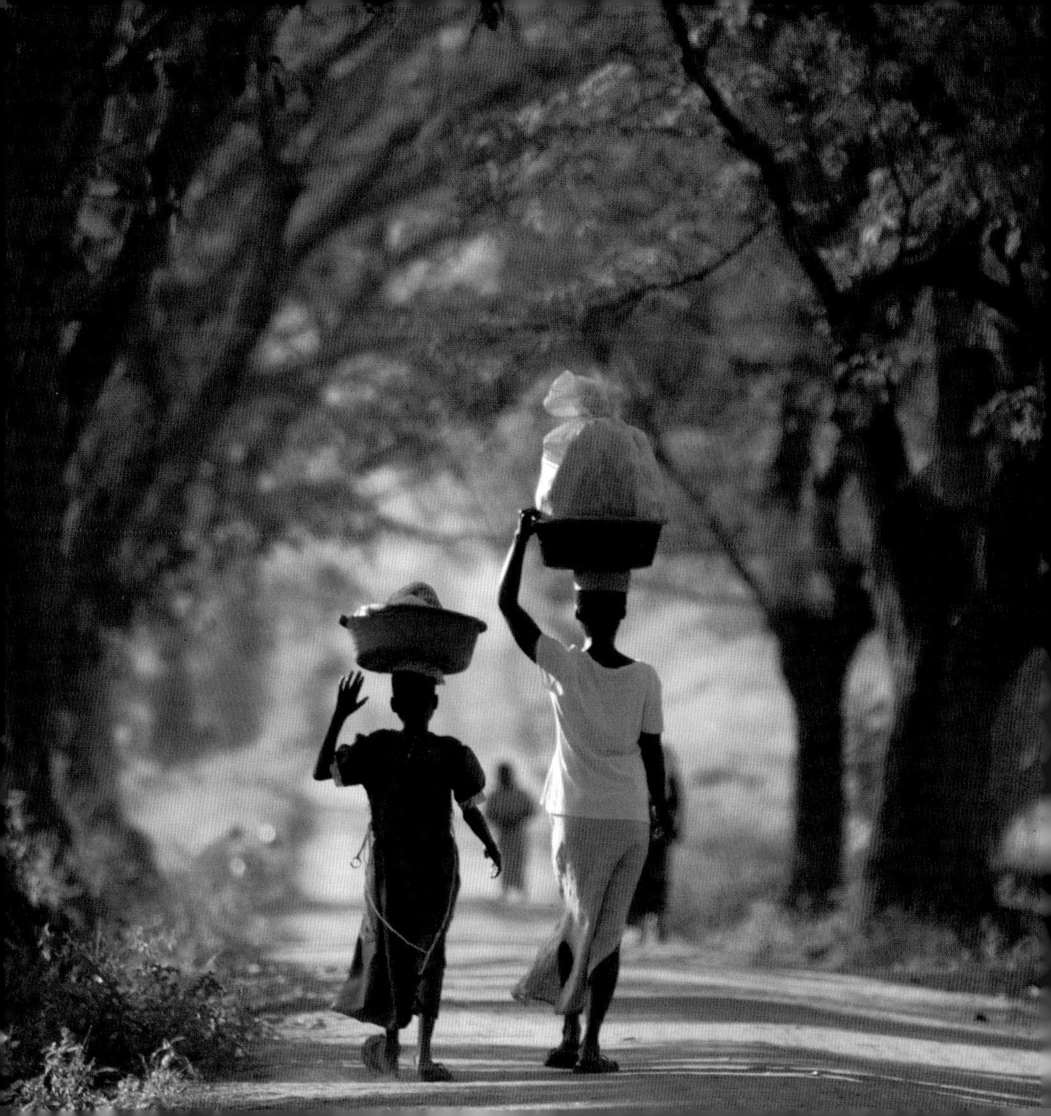

A sister is a friend

your heart chooses.

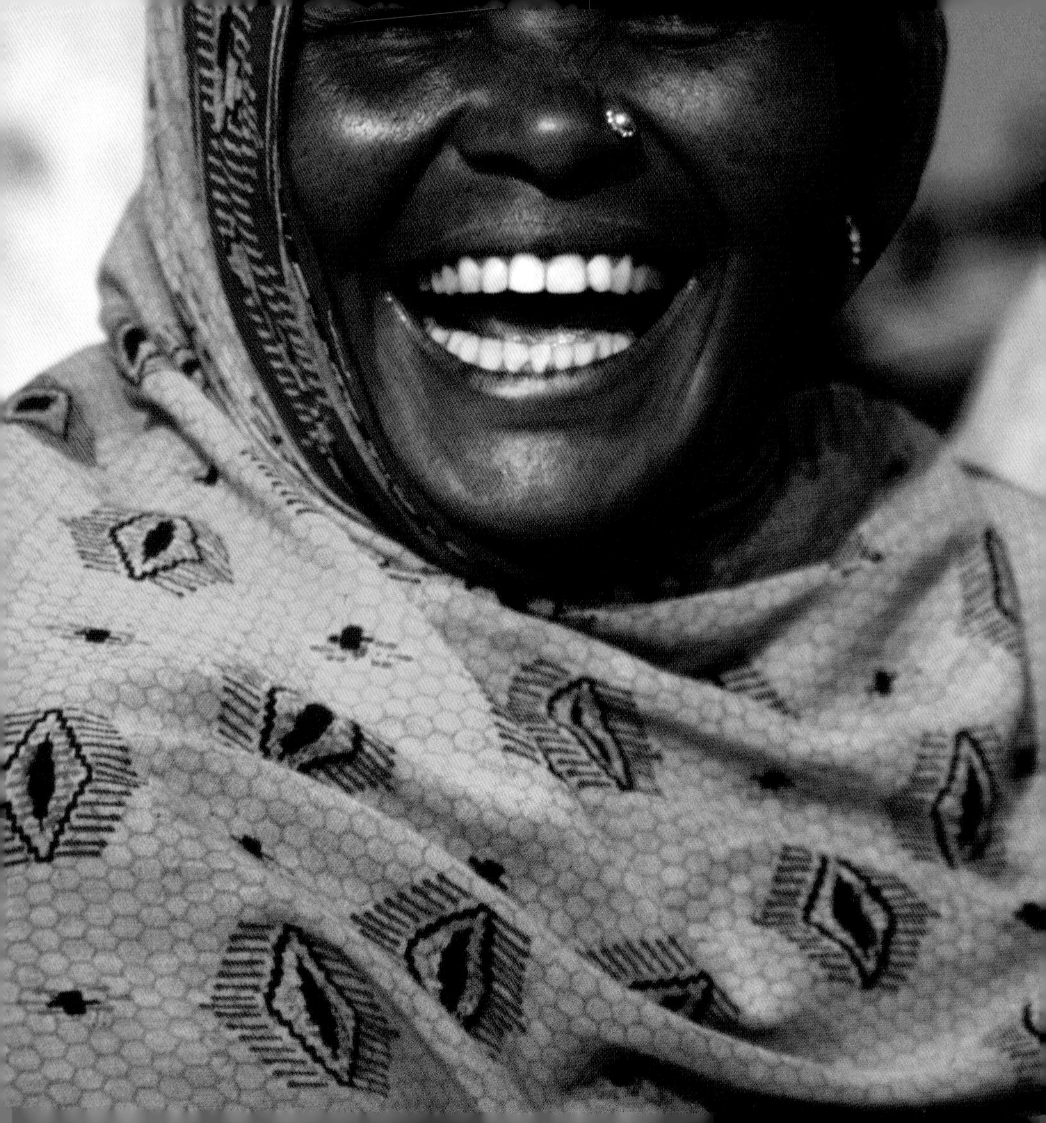

There is

something beautiful

about finding one's
inner most thoughts
in another.

...someone who knows

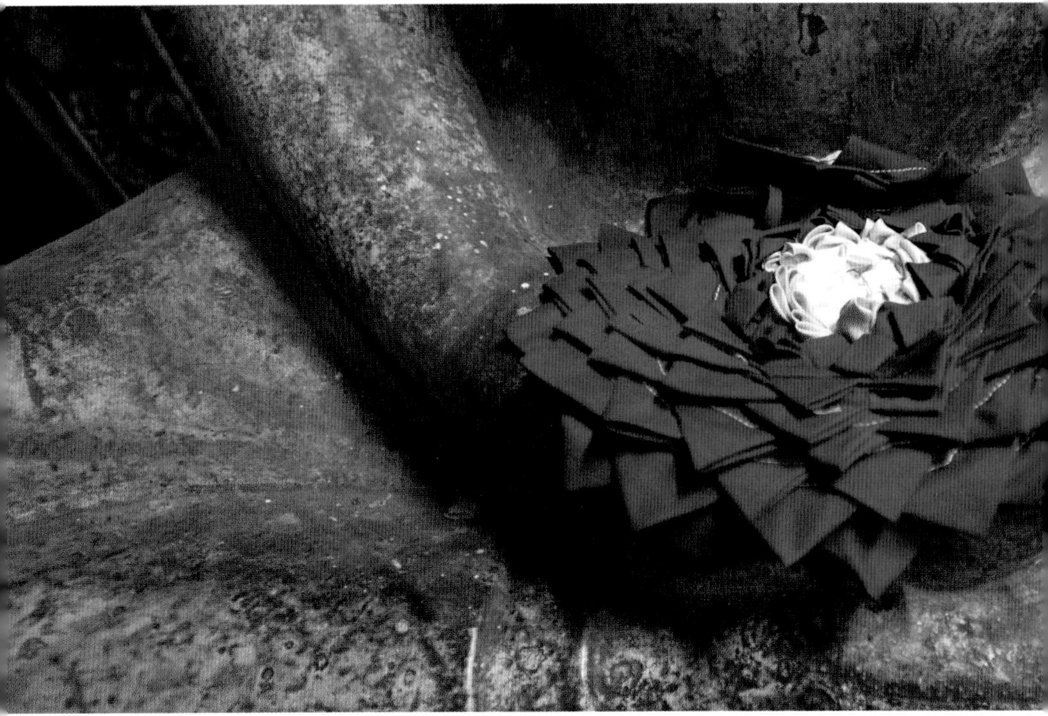

everything about you

and loves you anyway.

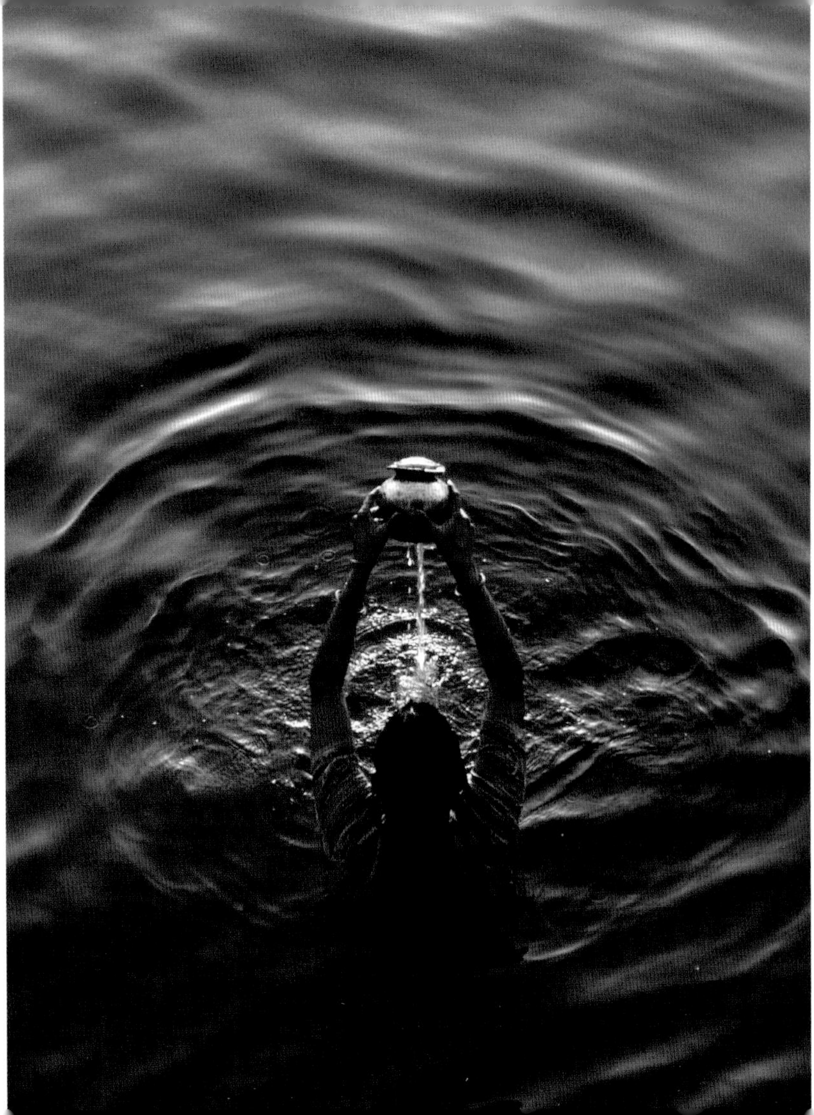

Let us
rise up
and be
thankful.

Buddha

A sister is
a gift to the heart,
a friend to the spirit,
a golden thread
to the meaning of life.

Isadora James

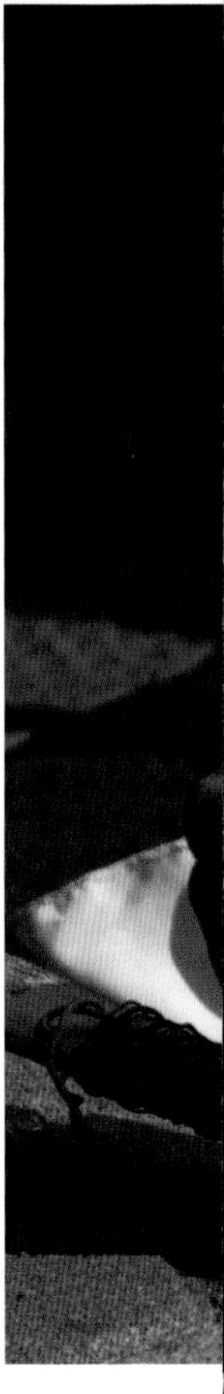

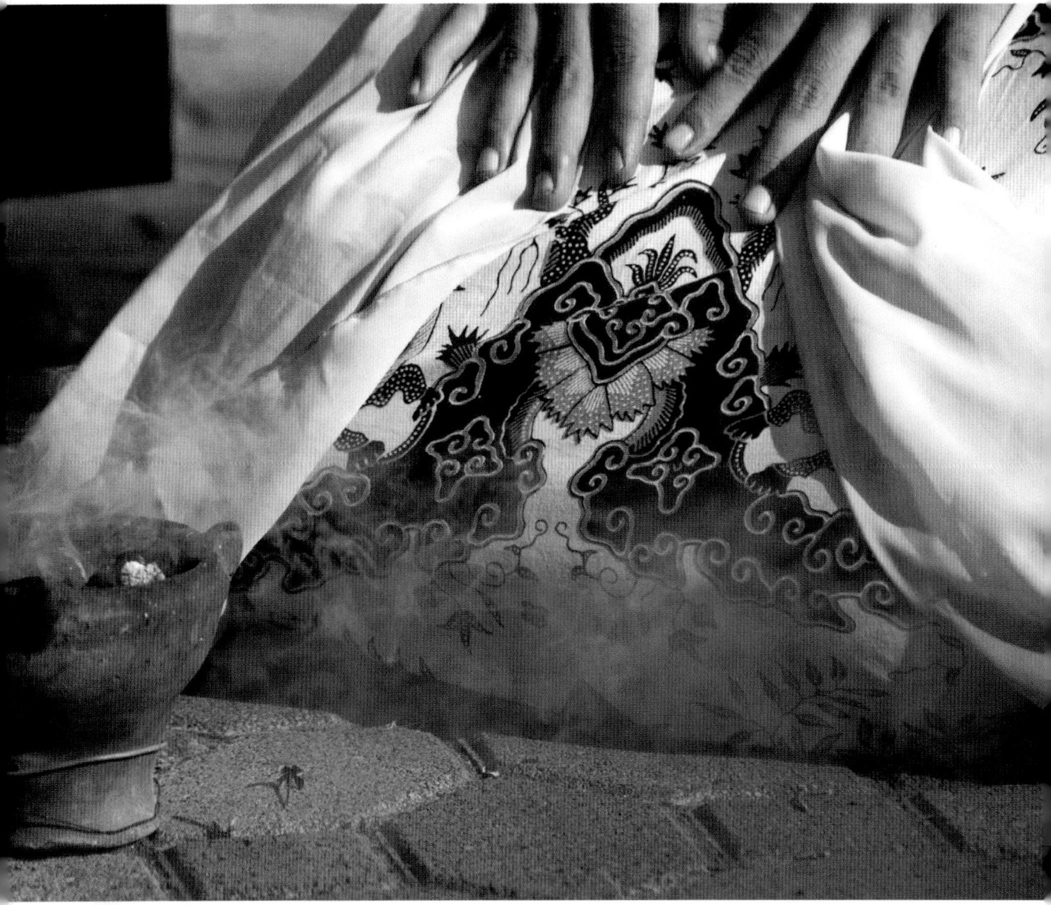

All that is in the heart
is written in the face.

African Proverb

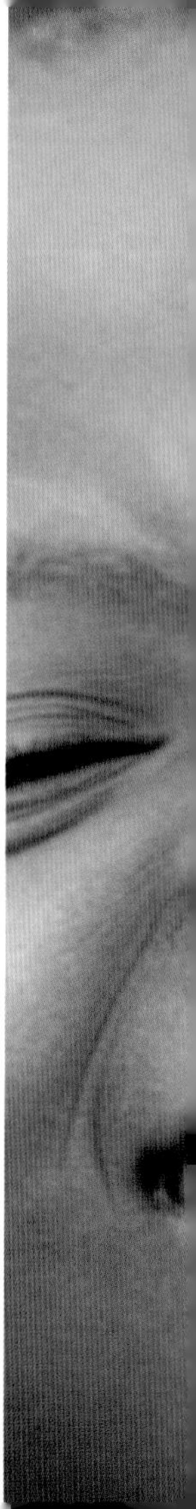

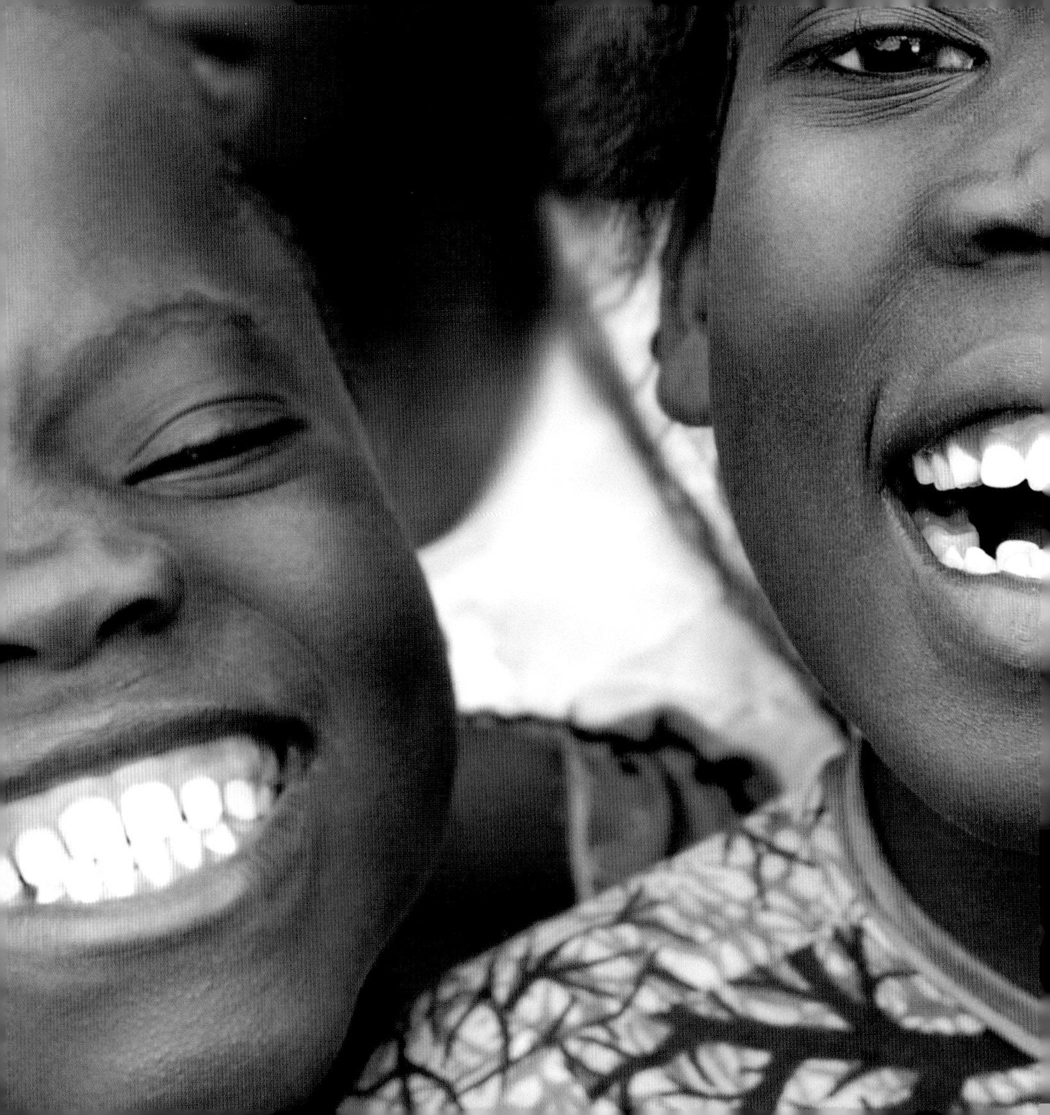

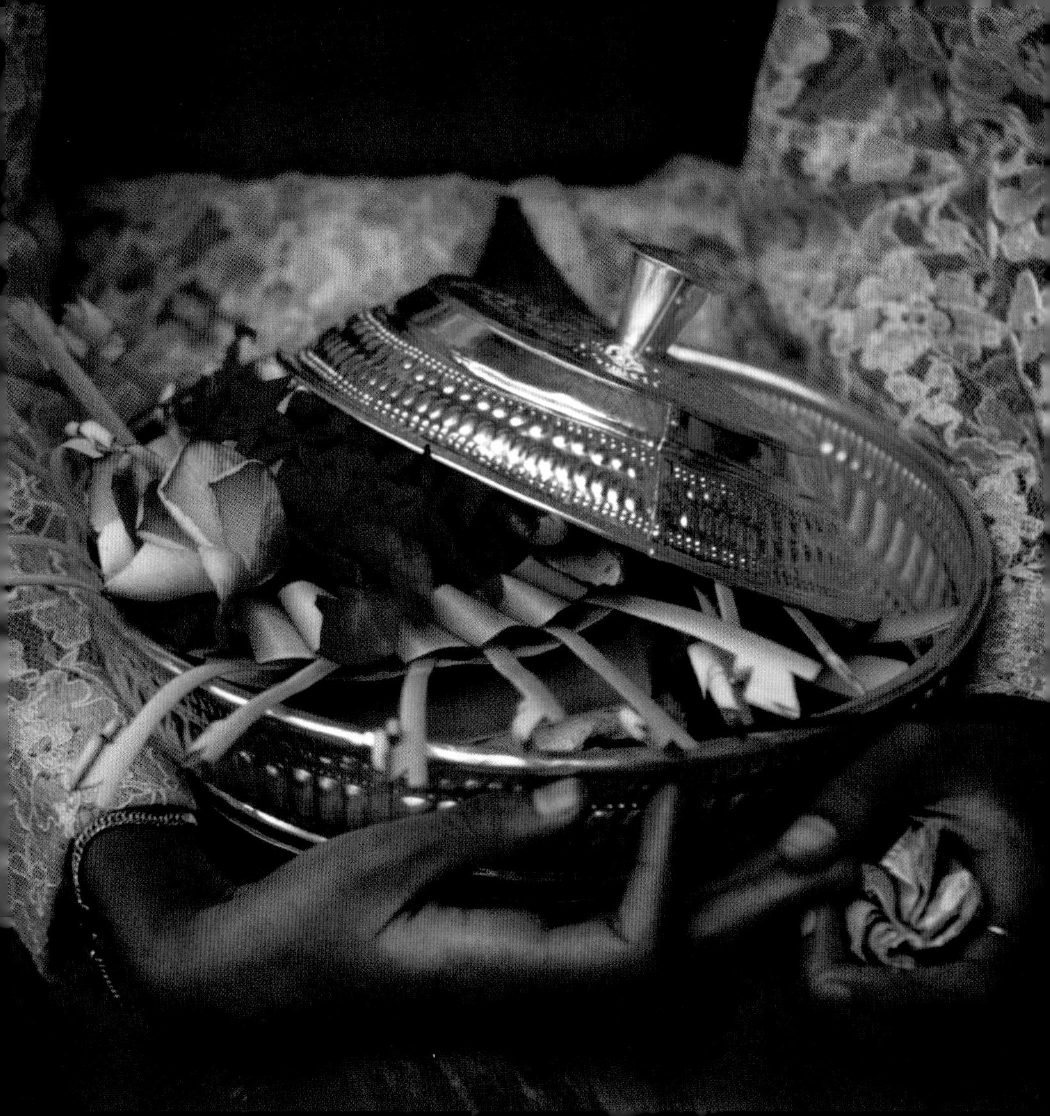

We see
magic and beauty
in things.
But the magic and beauty
are really
in ourselves.

Kahlil Gibran

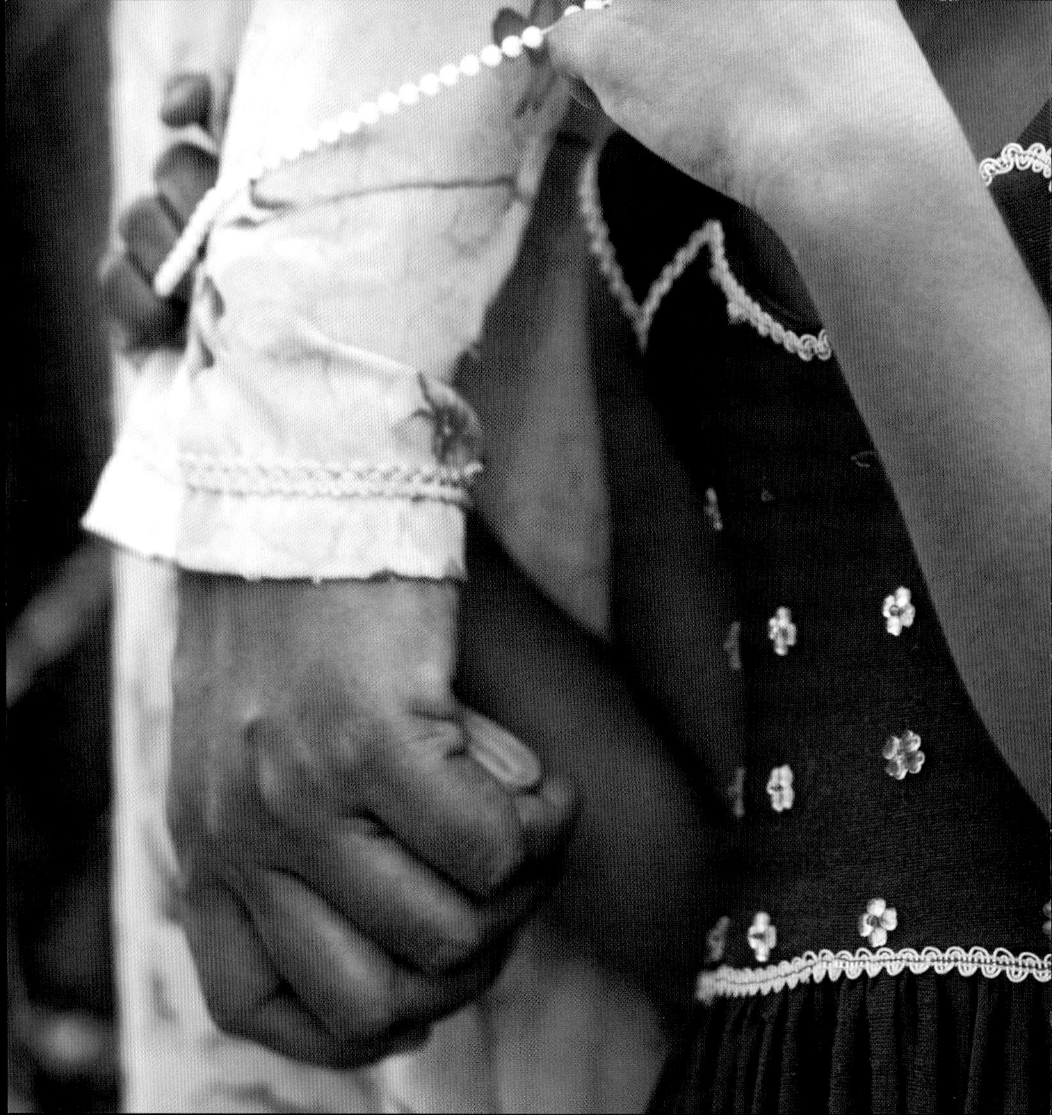

Love is
all we have,
the only way
that each
can help
the other.

Euripides

Each happiness
of yesterday

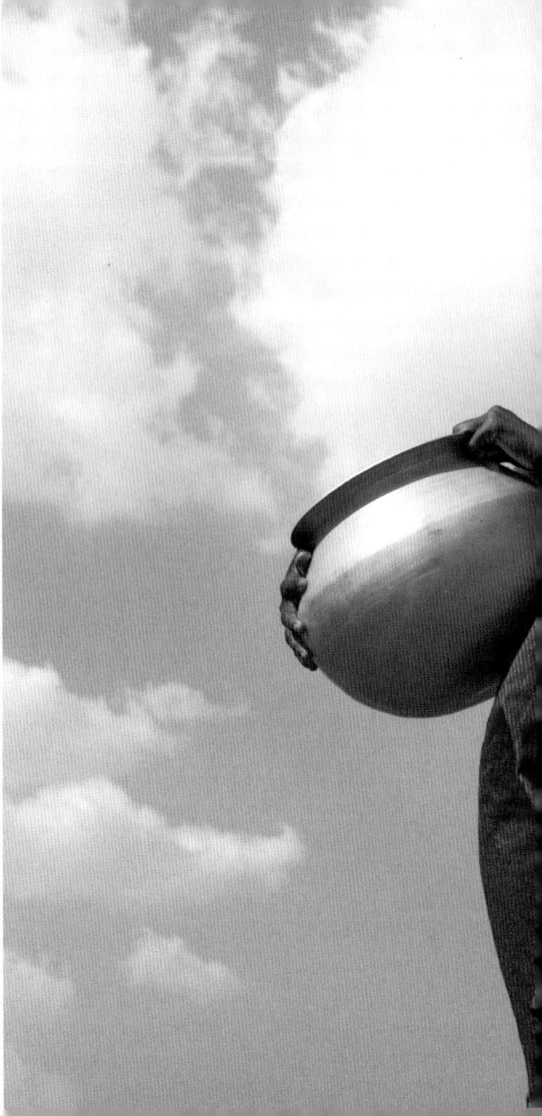

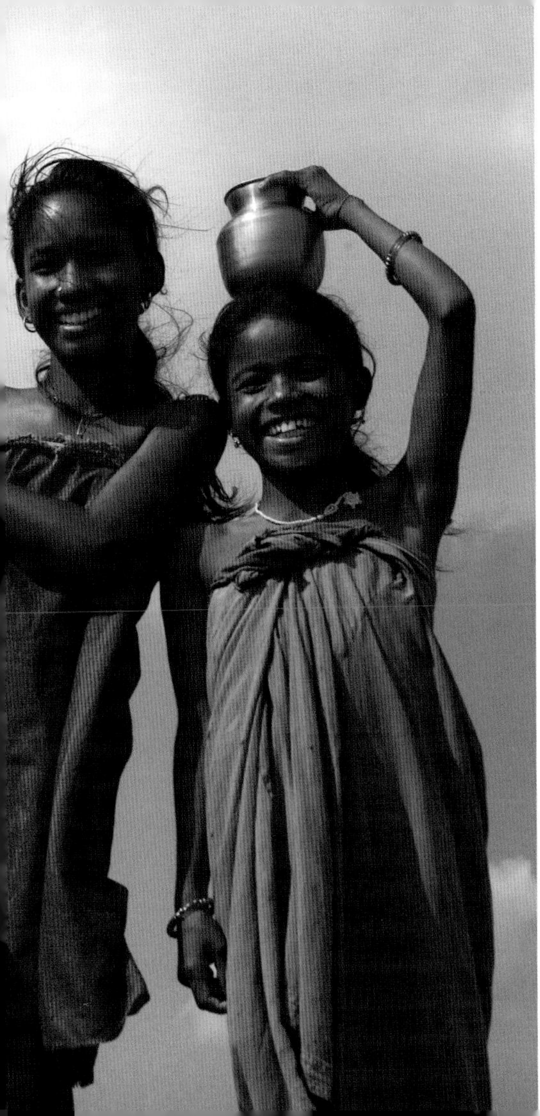

is a memory
for tomorrow.

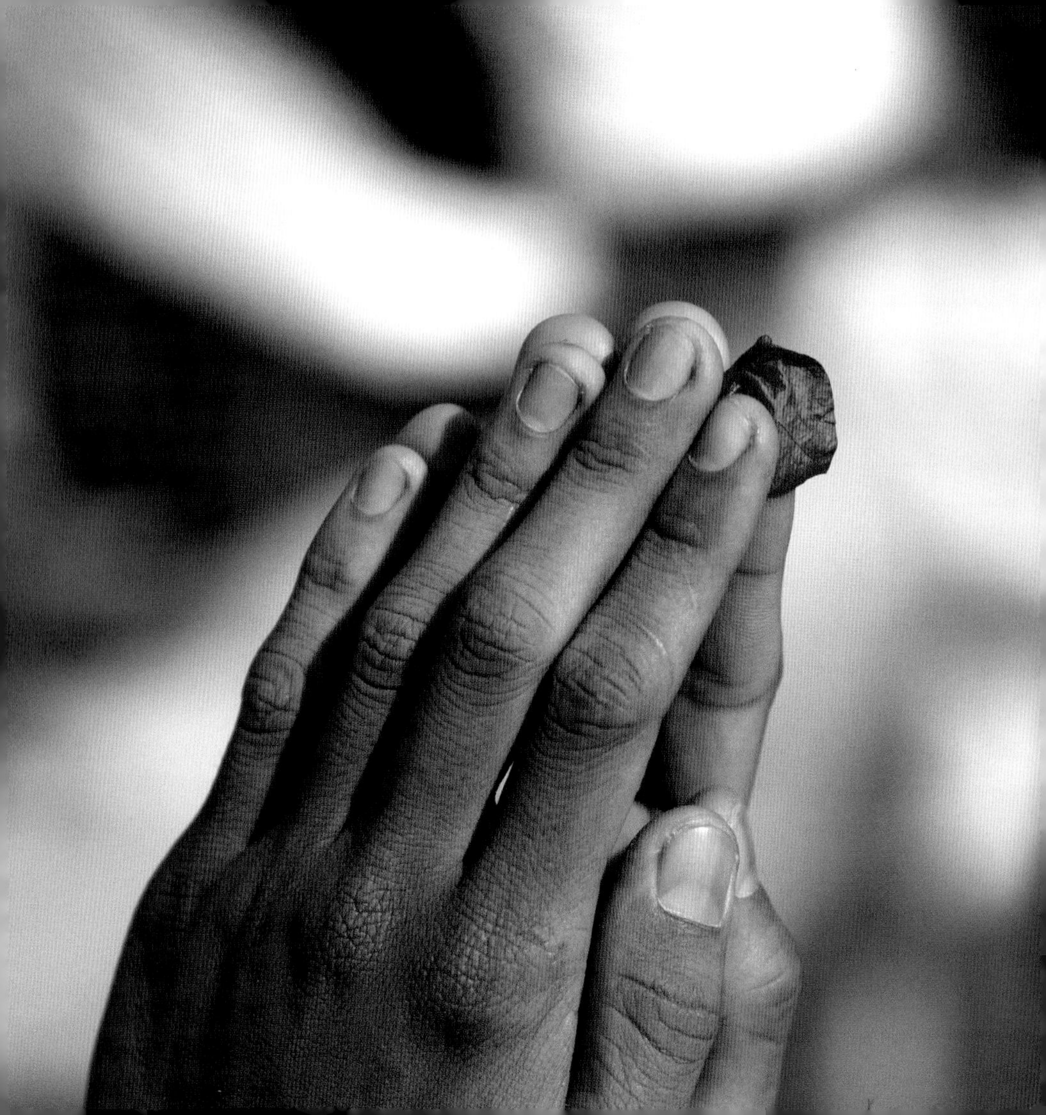

Sisters are

blossoms

in the garden
of life.

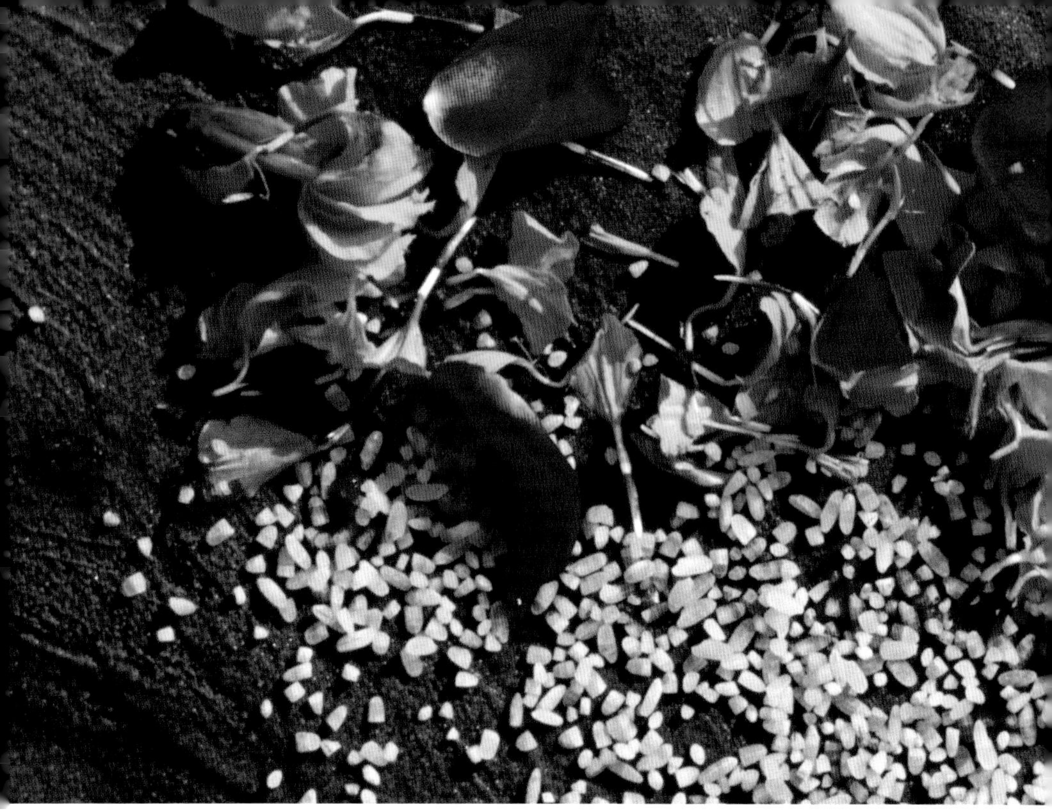

Individually unique.

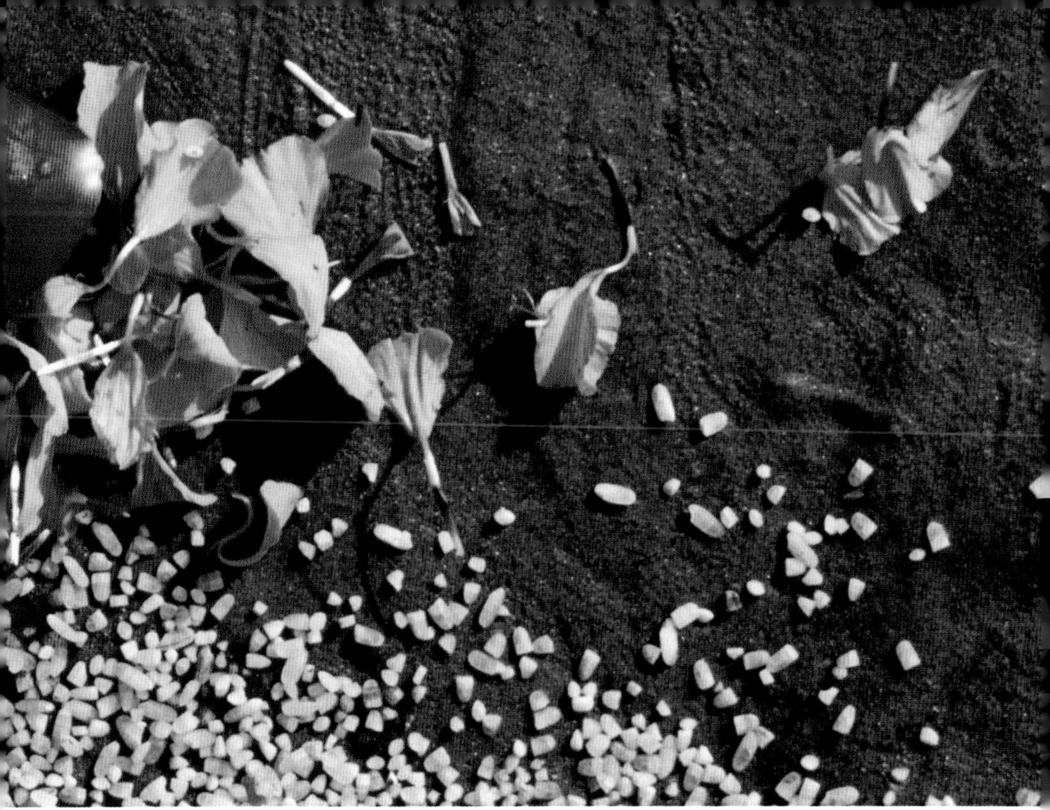

Together complete.

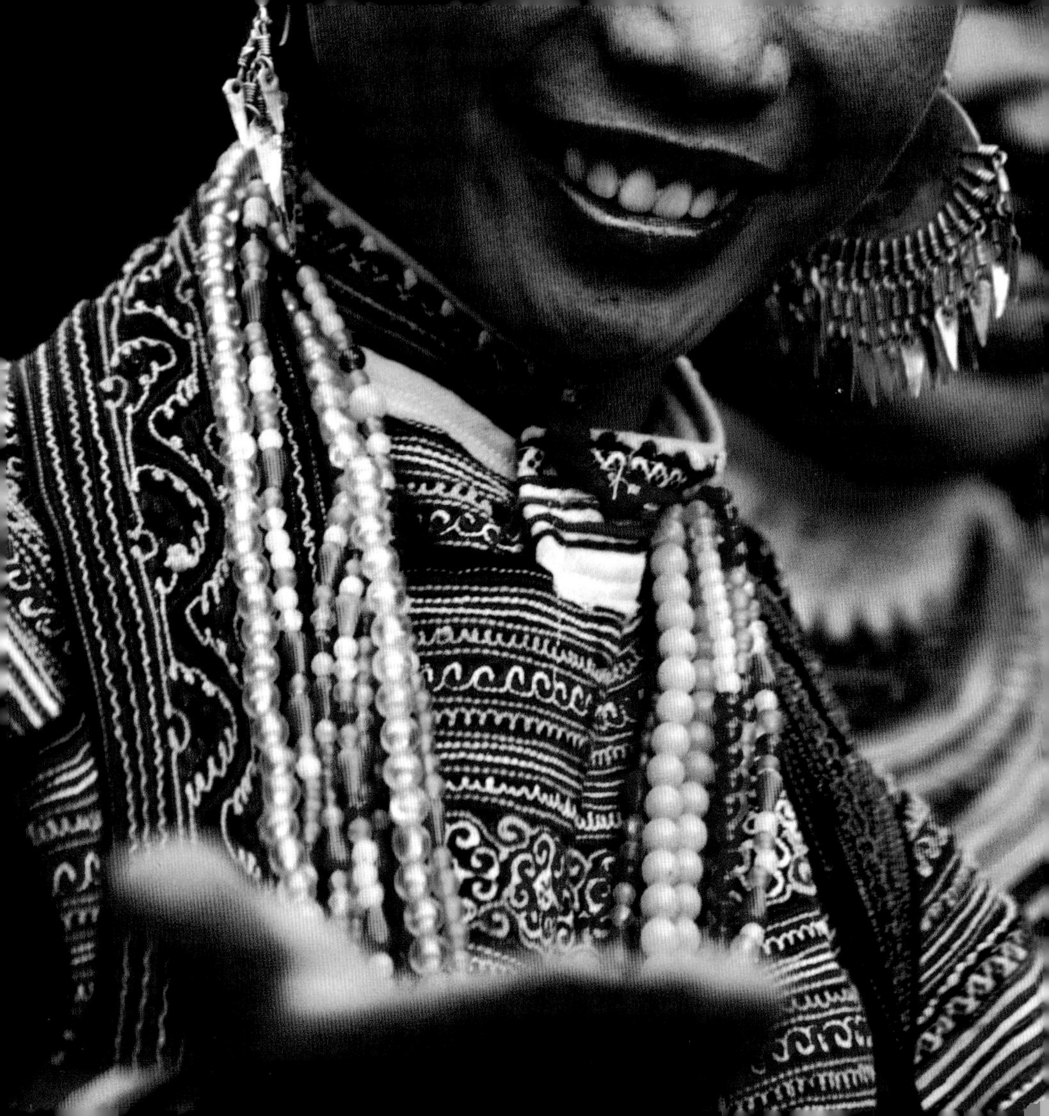

Bless you, my darling,
and remember
you are always
in the heart of
your sister.

Katherine Mansfield

bless you my darling

Other books by Affirmations Publishing House:

visit www.affirmations.com.au

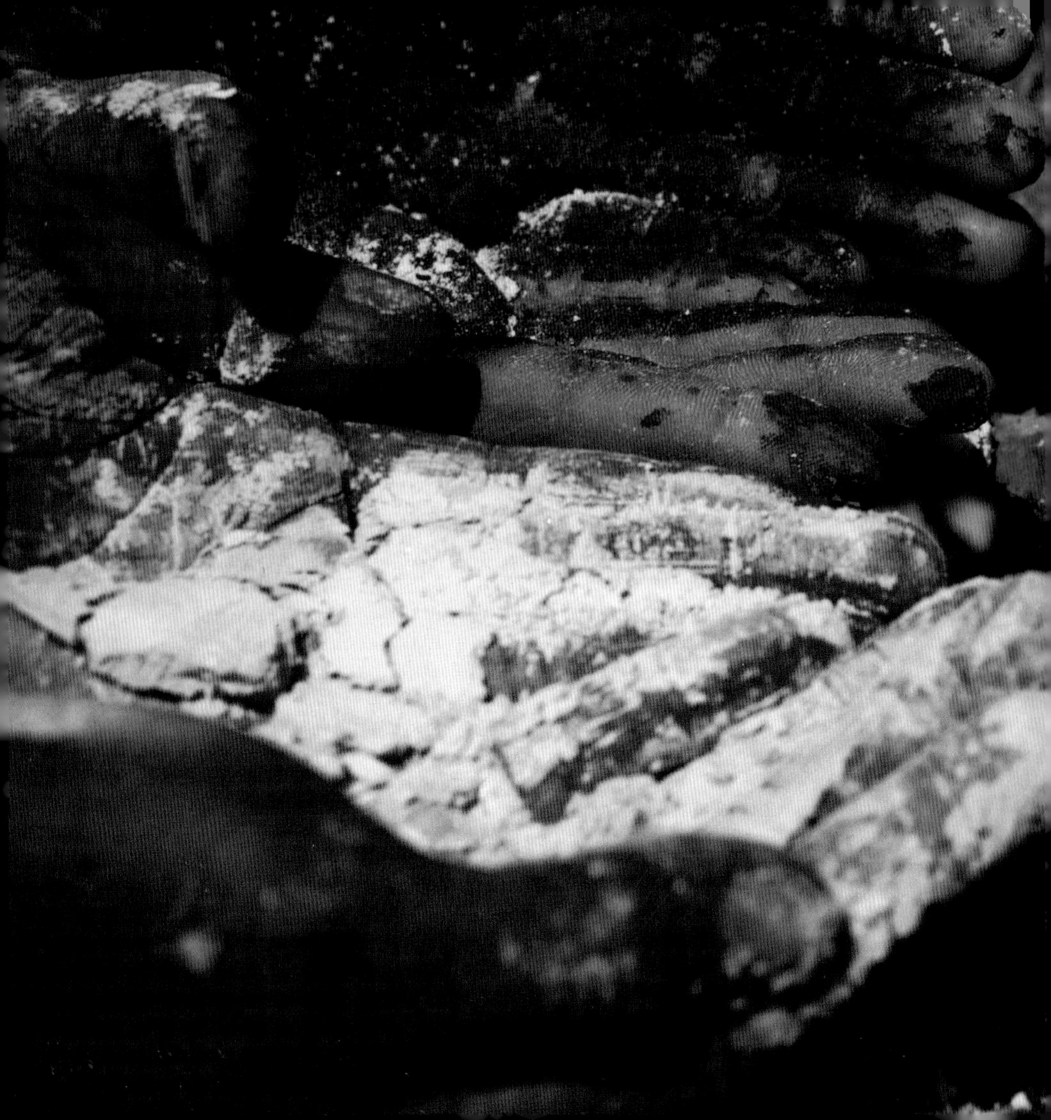